D1215446

Canadian Heritage Quilting
Quick, Creative Designs

Karen Neary and Diane Shink

Formac Publishing Company Ltd.,
Halifax

Copyright 2008 Formac Publishing Company Limited

All rights reserved. No part of this publication may be reproduced or transmitted in any form or by any means, electronic or mechanical, including photocopying, or by any information storage retrieval system, without permission in writing from the publisher.

Formac Publishing Company Limited acknowledges the support of the Cultural Affairs Section, Nova Scotia Department of Tourism, Culture and Heritage. We acknowledge the financial support of the Government of Canada through the Book Publishing Industry Development Program (BPIDP) for our publishing activities.

Design: Marianne Lohnes

Library and Archives Canada Cataloguing in Publication

Shink, Diane
    Canadian heritage quilting: quick creative designs / Diane Shink and Karen Neary.

ISBN 978-0-88780-753-4

    1.II. Title.
TT835.S4658 2008   746.46'041
C2008-903846-0

Formac Publishing Company Limited
5502 Atlantic Street
Halifax, Nova Scotia B3H 1G4
www.formac.ca

Printed in China

Acknowledgements

Pattern Instruction: Karen Neary   Historical Information: Diane Shink

We are grateful for the generous support of family and friends during the compilation of this manuscript. In particular we would like to thank pattern testers Lynn Bourgeois of River Philip, NS, and Alie Cameron of Antigonish, NS, for the many hours spent ensuring the accuracy of the patterns. The fabulous quilting on Log Canada, Redwork Strippy and Gram's Baptist Fan Quilt was done by professional longarm quilter Jacqueline Pohl of The Vintage Quiltery, Gladstone, Manitoba.

Special thanks to the following people and institutions who opened records and allowed access to data:
Peter Larocque, New Brunswick Museum, Saint John, NB
Scott Robson, Nova Scotia Museum, Halifax, NS
Lois MacDonald, Kings Landing, NB
Canadian Red Cross Society, Creations Quilters, Truro, NS
Colchester County Archives, Truro, NS
Fraser Cultural Centre, Tatamagouche, NS
Malagash Mine Museum, Malagash, NS
Mount Allison University Archives, Sackville, NB
Parkdale Maplewood Museum, Lunenburg County, NS

Textile Museum of Canada, Toronto, ON
David Dewer, Wallace and Area Museum, Wallace, NS
Westmorland Historical Society, Sackville, NB
Valerie Osborne, Nova Scotia Agriculture College, Truro, NS
Women's Institute, Truro, NS
Janet Bryson, Saint John, NB
John Corey, Havelock, NB

Thanks to the following people for lending quilts or related objects for photography:
Emily Drysdale, Montréal, QC
Nancy Fraser, Onslow Mountain, NS
Barb Ross Mackenzie, Cape John & Dartmouth, NS

Myrna MacPherson, Little Harbour, NS
Sammy Treen, Tatamagouche, NS
Chris Sonntag, Dartmouth, NS
Ruth & Art Weatherby, Truro, NS

Thanks to the following people for opening their homes as locations for photo shoots:
Heather Dyble, John Hastey, Sheila Graham, Ralph Belliveau and Lismore Sheep farm, River John, NS

Photographers:
Alex Brzezinski, Marilyn Greshorne, Morrow Scott Brown, Rob Johnstone, Karen Neary

Photographic Assistants:
Patrick Neary, James Neary
Computer consultation:
Rosemarie Smith, Philippe Shink, Darren Spidell

Editing Assistance:
Virginia Eisemon, Ann Catherine Lowe, Ellen Giles Millard, Peter Neary, Anne Scott Kaufman

Websites sourced:
http://images.rom.on.ca/public/index.php
http://www.mccord-museum.qc.ca/en/collection/artifacts/M972.3.1&section=196

Contents

Introduction

This book is intended to give a limited overview of the history of quilting in the Atlantic Provinces using illustrations from private and public collections. Quilting has become increasingly popular in the past decades and this book will show you how to make heritage-inspired quilts using 21st-century fast-and-easy methods. With the exception of Diane Shink's "In Apple Blossom Time" these popular patterns have been created by Karen Neary.

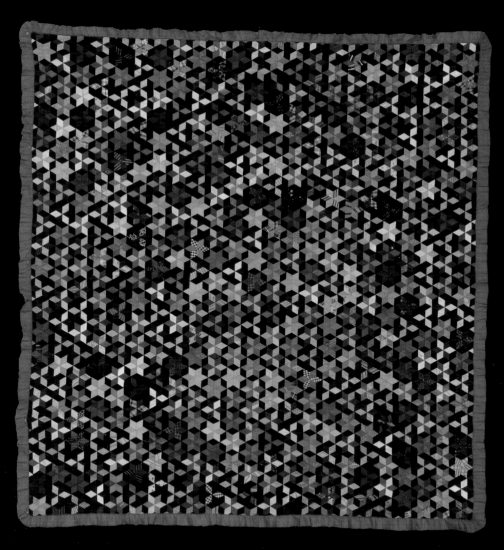

Silk 19th century paper-pieced star
70" x 80" (178 x 203 cm)

A quilt consists of three layers of material; the usually decorative top layer is placed over filling or batting with material for backing or lining, held together by stitching. Quilts were traditionally used as bed covers, those over one hundred years old are antiques and those half that age are considered to be vintage.

The earliest quilts, c. 1800, found in the Atlantic Provinces were made with homespun wool. Sheep were kept during these early days and their wool was used for utilitarian wool quilts, which kept many bodies warm on the long cold Canadian winter nights before centrally heated homes. Cotton and silk yard goods, imported from Europe through major seaports, were always available for a price. The silk star quilt (facing page) was hand-pieced in Halifax, NS, in the late 19th century. The oldest documented patchwork in North America dated 1726 and brought by British immigrants, was made of silk in the paper-pieced method. It is housed at the McCord Museum of Canadian History in Montreal.

The quilting tradition has always been strongest in the rural areas of Atlantic Canada. The earliest settlers grew flax in our maritime climate on newly cleared land, and home industries included textile production of linen as well as wool. At this time, before the Industrial Revolution, most of the family's needs were produced at home. A few references to quilt making have been located in diaries, but it was simply considered one of the many duties of a housewife, along with washing dishes and preparing food.

In the Atlantic Provinces the term quilting party rather than quilting bee was preferred to describe the working parties held when neighbours gathered in homes to quilt. These social times,

Quilting party print, 1934, by Violet Gillett, NB Museum

when women helped each other finish a quilt, usually included a group meal. Quilters sat around the frame that consisted of pieces of wood, two long and two shorter, held together by "C" clamps. The hostess would have prepared the top and assembled the backing and filling and possibly marked quilting designs in preparation for quilting. Wooden boards were sometimes carved with common quilting designs, such as cables, and used to stamp the design on the top with chalk.

Women always liked to share their work and exchange ideas, which included displaying

Hand-forged "C" clamps and pine quilting stamp, NB Museum

at exhibitions and fairs. It is not known if quilts were exhibited at the first known agricultural fair held in Nova Scotia at Windsor in 1765. Records from the Nova Scotia newspaper, *The Antigonish Casket,* report that 13 patchwork bed quilts were part of an 1863 exhibition. In Sackville, NB, in 1880, the Westmorland Agricultural and Emigrant Society Prize List included categories for patchwork quilts, silk and others.

Cotton was the material of choice for quilts made in the Atlantic Provinces, but the

plant needs more heat and a longer summer than we have so the fibre always had to be imported. The first and largest cotton mill in Canada was built in Marysville, NB, in 1861. The tariff on cotton goods imported into Canada was substantially raised in 1879, thus creating a burst of activity in textile manufacturing in Atlantic Canada. Today the manufacture of cotton yard goods has moved "offshore" because of prohibitive labour costs, leaving our cotton textile industry practically non-existent.

Making a quilt is a creative process starting with basic decisions about pattern selection, colour scheme and fabric choices. We have tried to guide you through the decision-making steps that help you make a quilt, be it large or small.

Left: Cotton bolls
Right: Westmorland Exhibition programme cover

General Directions

Basic sewing tools required for projects in this book are: a sewing machine in good working order, needles for hand sewing, thread, pins, scissors, rotary cutter, ruler and mat, marking tools such as pencils or water-soluble markers, measuring tape and iron.

MEASUREMENTS USED IN THIS BOOK: In Canada, we purchase fabric in metric units, but do our sewing with tools marked in Imperial measurements. The material requirements were calculated in metric and converted to the closest practical Imperial equivalent to allow ample fabric to complete the project (thus 1 m = 1-1/4 yards). We have written the instructions assuming that anyone using this book will be working in inches.

SEAM ALLOWANCE: All seam allowances are 1/4". Seam allowances are usually pressed to one side, towards the darker fabric.

WOF: This stands for "width of fabric." Fold the fabric in half, matching selvedge edges, and then fold in half again to meet the fold at the selvedge edge. Place your ruler across this width and cut a strip the desired width.

FABRIC SELECTION & PREPARATION: Most of the projects in this book are made using 100% cotton, which is sold in Canada by the metre. Pre-washing fabric is a personal choice, but for quilts that will see much washing (such as a child's quilt), it is recommended that all fabrics be washed before sewing.

THREAD: Use a good-quality cotton thread in a neutral or matching colour.

BATTING: Polyester battings are widely available and easy to quilt. Natural-fibre batts, such as cotton, silk and wool, are also popular. Your choice will depend on the look you prefer. Cotton generally has a lower loft, giving a more traditional look. It works especially well for placemats and table toppers. You may prefer a higher-loft polyester batt to give more definition to your quilting. In this book, the actual size of the batting required has been given, rather than simply "crib", "double" or "queen," as some batting is sold by the metre.

FOUNDATION PIECING: Foundation piecing allows you to accurately and quickly piece quilt blocks. All blocks include a 1/4" seam allowance around the completed piece, which is shown on the patterns as a light dotted line. The darker inside lines are sewing lines. The fabric pieces do not need to be cut precisely; you will trim them as you stitch. Make sure your pieces are at least 1/4" bigger on all sides than the section on the pattern that they will cover. Set your machine to a short stitch length, about 12–16 stitches per inch. Stitch with the right (marked) side of the paper facing up and the fabric underneath. Holding up the pattern to the light, place a piece of fabric right side out over section 1 on the plain side of the paper foundation (wrong side of fabric is next to the paper). Check to make sure that the section is covered by at least 1/4" of fabric all around. Secure with a pin. Place the fabric for section 2 right sides together with the first piece (you will sew along the seam line and then flip it to the right side, covering the marked section on the paper). Sew on the line between piece 1 and 2, beginning and ending a few stitches beyond either end of the line. Trim the seam allowance to a scant 1/4", flip the new piece to the right side and press the fabric open. Continue adding pieces to the foundation in numerical order until all the sections are covered. Trim the block to size by cutting on the outside

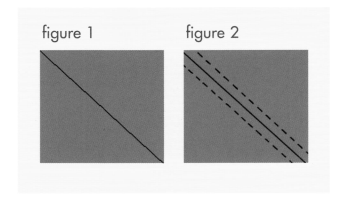

figure 1   figure 2

(light) dotted line. Sew appropriate sections together to form blocks. When it is time to remove the paper foundations, do so very gently so as not to pull the stitching out. Running a darning needle along the side of the stitches to score the paper first will help in the removal.

HALF-SQUARE TRIANGLES: Two triangles sewn together to make squares are called half-square triangles (HST). There are several ways to sew HST. The method used in this book is as follows: Cut your square 1" larger than the size of your finished square. For example, if a 2" finished block is desired, you will start by cutting a 3" square. Place one 3" square on top of another 3" square. With a pencil, draw a line diagonally from corner to corner. (figure 1) Stitch 1/4" on both sides of the drawn line. (figure 2) Cut apart on the line, open up the squares and press open. Measure and trim your block to 2-1/2" — which is a 2" finished block.

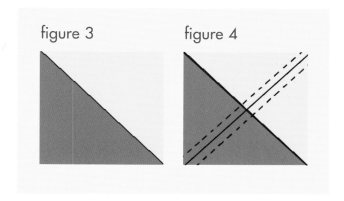

figure 3   figure 4

QUARTER-SQUARE TRIANGLES: To make quarter-square triangles (QST), squares are cut 1-1/4" larger than the finished size desired. Begin by making two HST as directed above. (figure 3) Place one HST

figure 5

on top of another, right sides together, with colours heading in opposite directions. (A blue triangle will be facing a yellow triangle.) Snug the seams together and pin. Draw a line diagonally from the corners opposite the first seam. (figure 4) Sew 1/4" on both sides of the drawn diagonal line. Cut the sewn unit in half on the drawn line. Press open. (figure 5) If you began with a 3" square, trim these blocks to 2-1/4", for a 1-3/4" finished block.

ADDING BORDERS: Borders may be butted at the corners, or mitred. For economy, fabric border strips are usually cut across the WOF. You may need to cut two strips of each width and seam them together on the short ends to achieve the correct length. To determine the length of your borders, measure your quilt top through the centre from top to bottom, going from raw edge to raw edge. Cut your border strips this length (at the width stated in the instructions) and sew them to the sides of your quilt. Now measure across the centre of your quilt from side to side, including the borders you just added. Cut your top and bottom border strips this length (at the width stated in the instructions). If you need to piece the border strips to achieve the proper length, centre this joining seam when sewing borders to your quilt top.

To make mitred corners on your borders, measure your quilt top as before (all four sides) and add double the width of your border + 6" to determine the length to cut your strips. Start at the centre of one side of your quilt and stitch, beginning and ending stitching 1/4" from each end. Repeat for all sides. Fold the fabric border strip into a 45° mitre at each corner; press. Open up the fold, realigning the edges as before with the borders, right sides together and pin. Stitch on the pressed line. Trim the seam allowance to 1/4". Mitred corners lie best if they are pressed open.

PIECING THE BACKING: Cut the backing and batting approximately 6" bigger all around than the quilt top. Trim threads and press your top and backing well before layering. The backing may have to be pieced for width. There are different ways to do this. The simplest way is to seam two pieces of fabric together and have the seam run vertically up the centre of the quilt back.

You may prefer to add width to each side of a centre panel of backing fabric to prevent a seam down the middle. Or, you may seam the fabric horizontally to have the seams running side-to-side, rather than up and down. When your backing fabric is ready, mark centres vertically and horizontally by folding fabric in half each way and marking with a safety pin.

BASTING: Basting is the process of securing the three layers of top, batting and backing together in preparation for quilting. Quilts may be secured by hand stitching or by using safety pins. Lay your backing fabric flat on a large surface, such as a table or the floor. The edges should be held taut; you can clip the fabric to a table using large binder clips, or the fabric may be secured to the floor with masking tape. Place the fabric right side down and make sure there are no wrinkles or folds in the fabric. Pull the fabric quite taut as you tape. On top of this, place your batting and smooth out any wrinkles. A piece of tape at each corner is usually enough to hold this. Mark vertical and horizontal centres on your quilt top the same as you did for the backing. Spread the

quilt on top of the batting, right side up, smoothing out as before. Match up safety pins on top and backing to make sure your top is centred on the backing. Tape the edges securely to the floor. With safety pins, pin all three layers of your quilt sandwich together, beginning at the center and working outwards to the edge of the quilt, leaving pins open until you are finished. Pins should be placed 4–6" apart. Check for any puckers in your quilt before closing all the pins. Roll up and quilt as desired.

When quilting is complete, trim outside edges of quilt evenly. Machine baste around outside edge of quilt, 1/8" from edge.

HANGING SLEEVE: If desired, a hanging sleeve may be added to the back of your quilt. This is done after quilting and before the binding is added. Measure the width of your quilt along the top edge. Cut a piece of fabric, this measurement x 6-1/2" wide. Turn under 1/4" twice on each short end of strip to form hem; stitch in place. Fold in half lengthwise, wrong sides together, and press. Centre this hanging sleeve on quilt, with the raw edge of sleeve placed at the raw top edge of the quilt. Pin; stitch along this edge. Hand-stitch the bottom (folded) edge of the sleeve to the back of the quilt. After the sleeve is stitched in place, proceed with the binding.

BINDING: Bindings may be straight-grain or bias. Choose a bias binding if your quilt has a curved edge (such as Gram's Baptist Fan quilt) or if the quilt will see much wear (such as the Ohio Star Baby quilt). Straight-grain bindings are quicker to make, and suitable for straight-edged wallhangings or placemats. All projects in this book use a French Fold (double) binding cut at 2-1/4" wide. This is not a magic number: you may prefer your bindings narrower or wider, but 2-1/4" is a good general width.

To make straight-grain binding, cut strips 2-1/4" x WOF. Seam together on short ends with a diagonal seam (to reduce bulk) if more length is required. Fold the strip wrong sides together along the length.

TO MAKE CONTINUOUS BIAS BINDING: Cut a 20" square of fabric. Cut square in half diagonally to form two triangles. Lay one triangle on top of the other and sew along top edge. (figure 6) Press seam open. Lay the fabric out and mark lines 2-1/4" apart on the wrong side. (figure 7)

Join the strip in a circle, matching the first line drawn to the second line drawn. Pin, and stitch. (This may seem wrong, but it isn't!) Press this seam open. (figure 8)

With scissors, begin at one end and cut on marked line. Fold the strip in half lengthwise as for straight-grain binding and press. (figure 9) A 20" square such as this, with binding cut at 2-1/4", will yield approximately 5-1/2 yards (5 m) of bias binding. Sew binding to the front edge of the quilt, mitering corners. Join ends. Fold binding to the back of the quilt and hand-stitch in place.

As with any work of art, it is important to sign your work. Add a label to the back that answers the questions who, what, when, where and why you made your quilt. Labels may be printed using the same method as in The Little Red Hen quilt, signed as in the Maple Leaf Signature quilt, or have the information hand-embroidered.

figure 7

figure 9

One-patch Quilts

One of the easiest ways to make quilt tops is to cut out same-sized squares of various colours of fabrics and sew them together. The method seen in the earliest quilts allows for easy recycling of fabrics and thus is economical. When cutting squares, a ruler and scissors were originally used to mark the straight lines, eliminating the necessity to use templates.

Many utilitarian quilts were made with wool since that material was produced and readily available in Eastern Canada. Narrow quilts were made from used clothing for the hired man's cot. Tailors' sample books provided rectangles for youth and trundle bed quilts. Even utilitarian-style quilts used attractive colour schemes, and recycled textiles such as drapes were used for backing. These heavy quilts were referred to as shore quilts on Prince Edward Island since they were used to keep the evening dampness away in camps by the salt water. Until recently, people on the Atlantic coast called these heavy wool quilts Fisherman's quilts.

One-patch quilt blocks can be arranged

Opposite: Hired Man's quilt — wool with drapery back

c.1940, 45" x 74.5" (114 x 190 cm)

in a number of ways, varying colours and lightness and darkness of shades to give different effects. Another popular method of adding interest is to embellish the squares by embroidering a design before the top is assembled.

variety of aprons to suit their wardrobes and activities. Made in many colours and designs, they not only protected the clothing but also provided a creative outlet. In pioneer days wool aprons were worn for safety when working around the open hearth, as wool is less likely to catch fire than cotton. Today vintage aprons are collector's items and patterns are again being printed.

Baby's quilt with embroidered stitching on each
8" (20 cm) block, c.1960, 41" x 54" (104 x 137 cm)

The green and white baby quilt with lines from the child's evening prayer, "Now I lay me down to sleep," is an example of this method. The more advanced quilter may wish to try arranging the blocks on point.

Squares can be used to make other household patchwork items such as aprons. These were a necessary part of clothing for housewives during most of the 20th century. When the supply of cotton became better, women used their imaginations to create a

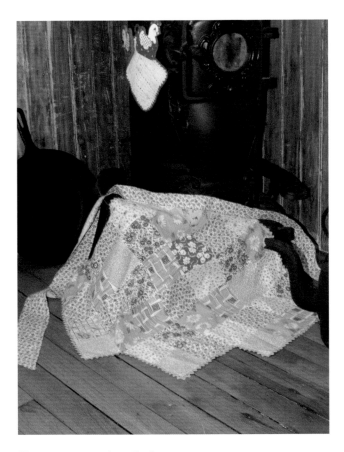

Vintage one-patch quilted apron
c.1950, 21" x 30" (53 x 76 cm)

14

One-patch Apron:
On Point Diagonal Set

This beginner apron pattern has the squares set "on point" to give interest to the design. The size may easily be adjusted by adding more squares and cutting the waistband a bit longer.

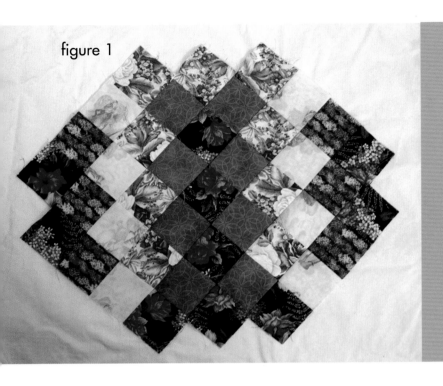

figure 1

Materials
45" (115 cm) wide cottons

- 0.25 m (1/3 yard) each of four different prints
- 0.6 m (5/8 yard) print (to be used for squares and waistband)
- 0.6 m (5/8 yard) lining fabric
- sewing thread to match

Finished size: 21" x 18"
Finished block size: 2-1/2"
Number of blocks required: 41

Cutting Instructions

From black print, cut two pieces 4-1/2" x WOF (these will be used for waistband ties)

From black print, cut 10, 3" squares.

From green print, cut 8, 3" squares.

From yellow print, cut 8, 3" squares.

From light floral, cut 9, 3" squares.

From striped floral, cut 6, 3" squares.

Directions

Lay out squares as shown and sew together in rows. (figure 1) Press seams to side.

Lay backing fabric right side up and place pieced apron right side down on top of the lining. (figure 2)

Sew around outside edges, leaving an opening spanning the three floral squares at the top.

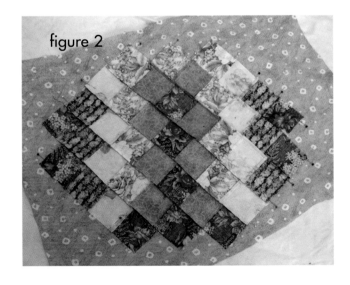

figure 2

Trim lining to within 1/4" of seam around the outside edges of the apron, clipping into corners to ensure a smooth edge when turned. (figure 3)

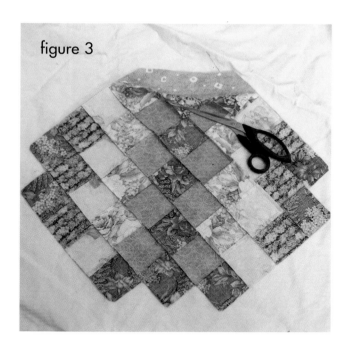

figure 3

Using ruler as a guide, trim 1/4" above centre on the 3 squares at the top of apron. (figure 4) Turn apron right side out through opening at top and press.

Sew short ends of waistband strips together; press seam to one side. Centre this seam on top of patchwork apron opening, right sides together, and stitch across top of apron. Fold waistband tie ends together along length with right sides together and trim ends in a 45° angle. Stitch to apron, break stitching at waistband and repeat for other tie end. Turn ties right side out and fold waistband over to the back side of apron. Slipstitch in place.

figure 4

Flannelette Nap Quilt: Straight Set

Simple quilts can be made any size from squares. This cozy one is made from flannelette.

Cutting Instructions

Cut a total of 70, 7" squares. Lay out 7 across and 10 down as shown. (figure 1)

A random arrangement of colours works best to give your quilt a "scrappy", old-fashioned look.

(figure 1)

Materials
45" (115 cm) wide cottons

- 0.5 m (5/8 yard) each of seven different prints — if using scraps, cut squares 7"
- 6 m (6-3/4 yards) binding or 0.5 m (5/8 yard) fabric for binding
- 1.8 m (2 yards) batting
- 3.6 m (4 yards) backing fabric (115 cm flannelette will need to be pieced for this width)

Finished size: 45.5" x 65"
Finished block size: 6-1/2"
Number of blocks required: 70

Directions

Sew squares in rows, then sew rows together. Press seams in each row in alternate directions.

Baste layers together. Machine quilt vertically and horizontally "in the ditch" (through joining seams), and diagonally through the squares. Bind.

Nine-patch Quilts

In a variation of the simple block, nine equal-sized squares are arranged in three rows of three to form a new block. This arrangement may have links to the Christian tradition with light and dark colour values used to form the shape of a cross.

Quilters of the past did not always give names to their patterns but referred to their quilts simply as "the green and white one" or "that patchwork made from leftovers of the girl's dresses." Pattern names varied regionally. Inland, a variation of the Nine-patch with half-square triangles was called *Hole in the Barn Door*, while on the Atlantic coast it was called *Fisherman's Reel*. The correct name is the one the maker gave it. Today for identification we have reference books for pattern names.

Scottish immigrants who settled high in the Cobequid Mountains of Nova Scotia used cradles to protect their infants from drafts and help establish sleep patterns, thus ensuring the child would live through infancy. The mid-20th century patchwork quilt in the cradle (below) was hand-pieced by a Nova Scotian while living in Kansas and group quilted when she returned home.

In the 19th century girls began instruction in the use of needle and thread by the age of three and practiced their skills by making samplers and doll quilts. In the musical *Anne of Green Gables*, based on the book by PEI author L. M. Montgomery, the red-headed heroine Anne is not allowed to go out and play until she has done her stint on her patchwork.

Sitting beside the kitchen stove in her

Opposite: Nine-patch variation Ship of Dreams, completed by Diane's mother in 1939, 65" x 75" (165 x 190 cm)

Cotton Nine-patch made by Lottie Treen using wool from her brother's sheep for batting, Malagash, NS, c.1935, 65" x 75" (165 x 190 cm)

Backing of an antique Nine-patch set on point

boarding house, Diane's mother often pieced quilt tops in the winter evenings. Her blue and white *Ship of Dreams* quilt dates from the 1930s and is well worn after many years of providing warmth for her only son.

Carding mills operated throughout the Atlantic Provinces during the 19th century to process the wool sheared from sheep. Homespun made on privately owned looms was narrow, so in most cases the lengths of wool were joined with a whipstitch to make the backing wide enough for a bed-sized quilt. These wool blankets were also used for wadding or filling and made the quilt very heavy. The backing of the antique Nine-patch set on point (shown below) is two narrow widths of homespun wool. It was purchased near Meteghan, one of the predominantly French areas of Nova Scotia. Heavily used, the fabric is worn and the cottons faded.

Below: Nine-patch, 58" x 72" (147 x 182 cm)

Lambent Nine-patch Quilt

This setting is called a Radiant Nine-patch, as the colours radiate from the centre out through each block. If you look closely, you will see that the gold used in the centre becomes the secondary colour in the first row of Nine-patch blocks alternating with the dominant cream colour. The cream carries into the next set of Nine-patch blocks as the secondary colour, and this pattern continues to the edge of the design.

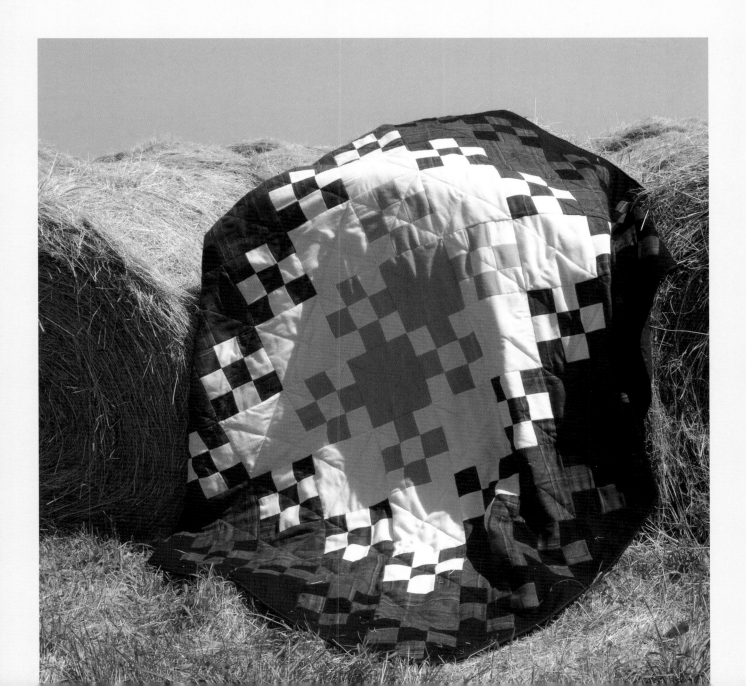

Lambent Nine-patch Quilt

Wool yardage is traditionally sold 60" (150 cm) wide; however some mills put it up at 54" (135 cm) wide. Check carefully when purchasing your wool. If you should decide to make this design using cotton, more yardage will be required to compensate for the narrower width of the fabric.

Working with wool presents some unique challenges to the quiltmaker, not the least of which is dealing with the weight and warmth of the top as it is being constructed. As it is bulky, seam allowances are pressed open rather than to the side. Being a loose weave, wool tends to fray on the edges and for this reason, we recommend that you clean-finish the edges of your strips and blocks before sewing them together. To do this, work a simple, long zigzag stitch along all cut edges of the wool using a regular sewing machine or serger. If using a serger, ensure that your cutting knife is disengaged so you don't trim any off the width of your strips. Press strips and squares flat after finishing the edges.

Batting is optional in a wool quilt. You may choose simply to back the quilt top with flannelette or plain cotton. If you do use batting, a very thin one, such as flannelette, is recommended. As a rule, wool quilts produced in the Maritimes did not have borders, so that tradition is reflected in this design. The name of the quilt is a play on words; "lambent" means "radiant" and seems appropriate as the quilt is made from lamb's wool.

Edges of wool, clean-finished before sewing

Cutting Instructions

Strips are cut across the WOF.

From gold, cut 2, 9-1/2" squares.

Cut 3, 3-1/2" strips across WOF.

From cream, cut 2, 9 1/2" WOF strips; recut into 10, 9-1/2" squares.

Cut 9, 3-1/2" strips x WOF.

From blue plaid, cut 3, 9-1/2" WOF strips; recut into 18, 9-1/2" squares.

Cut 11, 3-1/2" strips x WOF.

From black, cut 6, 14" squares; cut these squares diagonally into quarters to form the setting triangles along the outside edge.

Cut 2, 7-1/4" squares; cut these squares diagonally in half to form the 4 corner triangles.

Cut 5, 3-1/2" strips x WOF.

After cutting strips and squares, clean-finish all cut edges as directed above.

Directions

Press all seams open. Sew a gold strip between two cream strips to make Strip Set A, measuring 9-1/2" wide. Cut apart into 3-1/2" segments. (figure 1)

Materials
60" (150 cm) wide wool

- 1.5 m (1-2/3 yards) black
- 1.4 m (1-1/2 yards) cream
- 2 m (2-1/2 yards) blue plaid
- 0.6 m (5/8 yard) gold
- 5 m (5-2/3 yards) of 115 cm (45") wide flannelette for batting
- 5 m (5-2/3 yards) of 115 cm (45") wide flannelette backing
- 9 m (10 yards) bias binding or 0.6 m (5/8 yard) fabric
- Sewing and quilting thread to match

Finished size: 76-1/2" x 89"
Finished Block Size: 9"
Number of blocks required: 42 Nine-patch blocks, 30 One-patch blocks

figure 1

Sew a cream strip between two gold strips to make Strip Set B, measuring 9-1/2" wide. Cut apart into 3-1/2" segments. (figure 2) See next page.

figure 2

Sew one B segment between two A segments to make a block. Repeat to make 6 gold and cream blocks coloured like this:

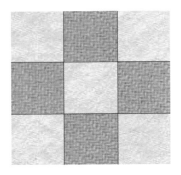

Using above method, make blue plaid and cream strip sets. Cut 28 blue/cream/blue segments and 14 cream/blue/cream segments. You will need 14 blue plaid and cream blocks coloured like this:

Sew blue plaid and black strip sets as above. Cut 44 black/blue/black segments and 22 blue/black/blue segments. You will need 22 blue plaid and black blocks coloured like this:

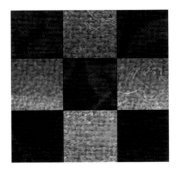

Blocks measure 9-1/2" square at this point. Press seam allowances open.

Lay out blocks diagonally as shown in sketch (figure 3), alternating plain blocks with pieced ones and placing black triangles along outside edges. Sew blocks together in rows, then sew rows together.

Press all seams open. Machine-stitch around outside edge of quilt to secure seams.

Layer top, batting, and backing. Baste. Machine-quilt diagonally through the seams. Bind quilt.

figure 3

Rail Fence Quilts

It is believed that the Rail Fence design (also called Roman Stripe) was a precursor for the Log Cabin design. The simple design consists of four or five rectangles or strips sewn together lengthwise into a block. In some cases these strips were torn so an industrious woman could construct this quilt even if she did not own a pair of scissors. Generally the direction of the strips is reversed in alternate blocks to add interest. This is a recommended design for beginning quilters, as all seams are straight lines. The antique quilt shown on the opposite page was constructed entirely of simple rectangles joined by hand, using a large variety of silk velvets in varying colours and values.

Diane's mother used dressmaking cuttings from the 1950s to repair a quilt made by her grandmother in the 1930s. The older quilt has a wool batt which had shrunk during many washings and now gives a shirred effect to the cotton strips.

Diane used the same print, alternating piece rectangles with white blocks, to make her first bed quilt entirely by machine in 1962. At that time the choice was between cotton or the

Diane's quilt, left, c.1962, 67" x 69" (170 x 175 cm)
Diane's mother's quilt, right, 65" x 75" (165 x 190 cm)

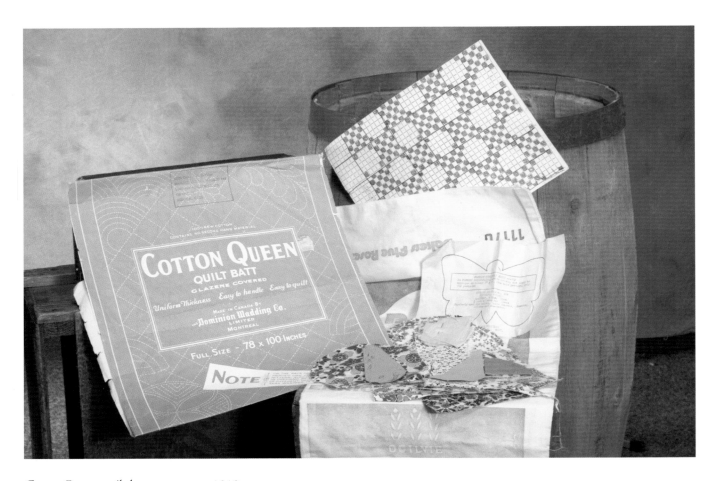

Cotton Queen quilt batt wrapper, c.1940

new synthetic polyester for filling. Polyester fibres, just being marketed in Canada, were more stable and resilient and did not require as much quilting. The company wrapped the new polyester batts in the same style as their Cotton Queen and still included a pattern on the inside. This clever marketing ploy allowed the quilter to start planning her next quilt while she was quilting the current one. If she did not

like the free pattern provided, a coupon was also part of the package, which in the 1940s encouraged her to send the coupon and 20 cents to the Dominion Wadding Company on Vinet Street in Montreal for any of the 38 available patterns.

Not everyone had the money to buy cotton quilt batts. The frugal housewife might have to use an older worn one as filling for a

*Full view of Velvet Rail Fence quilt with pink ruffled edging,
65" x 69" (165 x 175 cm)*

together. Some quilters load their needle, the shorter the better, with a number of stitches, rocking the needle back and forth through the layers. The stab stitchers take one stitch at a time going up and down. Many stories have been told of quilters removing stitches that were less than eight per inch after the offending quilter had left the party.

Hand-cranked sewing machine, c.1870

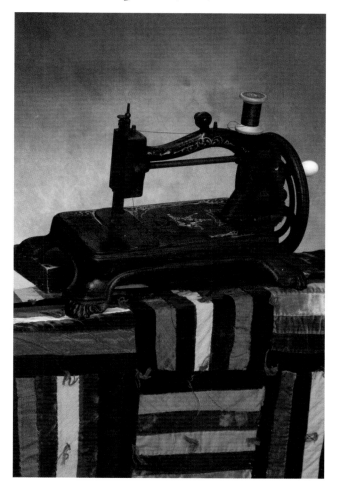

new quilt. Sometimes the quilting was not done until the maker was establishing her own household. Diane's mother purchased backing and batts to complete three tops the summer she was married. The quilting frame was set up in the orchard under the apple trees on the family farm. A few neighbours, known to be able to make even small stitches, were invited to come and assist. They made a running stitch through all thicknesses to hold the layers

Velvet Rail Fence Lap Quilt

*Diane's antique Velvet Rail Fence is updated using faster, strip-piecing methods. Use of an "even feed"
or "walking" foot on the sewing machine helps prevent the layers of velvet from shifting when stitching.
Seam allowances are pressed open to reduce bulk. The quilt is backed with a polished cotton
which is also used for the ruffle.*

Cutting Instructions

From velvet fabric, cut strips 1-1/2" x WOF
(approximately 70 strips).

From dark red, cut 10 strips 6-1/2" wide x
WOF. Set aside to make ruffle.

Directions

Sew 7, 1-1/2" wide velvet strips together
along long edges.

This strip set should measure 7-1/2" wide
when sewn. Colours are added in an even
pattern in each block from the centre

Materials
45" (115 cm) wide

- 4 m (4-1/2 yards) total of 7 different
  colours velvet or velveteen
- 1.8 m (2 yards) dark red cotton for ruffle
- 3 m (3-1/4 yards) backing
- 6 m (6-3/4 yards) thin cord — like
  crochet cotton — for gathering the ruffle
- Sewing thread to match
- 1 skein black 6-strand embroidery cotton
  for tying
- Curved needle (optional — but makes
  tying easier)
- 6 m (6-3/4 yards) of 1/8" black satin
  ribbon
- Large-eyed needle (for threading the satin
  ribbon under the cotton loops)

Finished Size: 42" x 56" + ruffle
Block size: 7"
Number of blocks used: 48

outward — e.g. start with blue, add a red to each side, add a purple to each side of the reds, then add a black to each side of the purples. Press seam allowances open. Cut the strips into 7-1/2" lengths. Each strip set should yield 5 blocks; you will need 10 strip sets to give 48 blocks.

Lay blocks out as shown, 6 blocks across and 8 blocks down. (figure 1) Sew together in rows, then sew the rows together. Press seams open.

To make the ruffle, sew the dark red strips together on short ends to form a loop. Press joining seams open. Fold long strip in half with wrong sides together and press. Lay crochet cotton on raw edge of ruffle a scant 1/4" from edge and set machine to a long, wide zigzag stitch. Stitch over the crochet cotton, encasing it with the zigzag stitches, around the entire edge of fabric. Divide fabric strip into quarters, mark with a pin. Find centre of each side of quilt top and mark with pins. Place ruffle on quilt top, matching pins

on ruffle with pins on the quilt top and having raw edges of ruffle even with the outside edges of the quilt. Pin together at these spots, and draw up cord to gather ruffle. Distribute gathers evenly and pin in place around perimeter of quilt. Stitch around entire outside edge.

Lay quilt top right side together with backing; pin, and stitch around outside edge leaving a 10" opening for turning. Turn right side out. Stitch opening closed with hand stitches and matching thread. Spread quilt out, pin baste as for quilting to hold layers together. With black embroidery cotton, thread the curved needle and make a stitch at the intersection where the blocks join. Leave about a 6" end, clip thread, and tie in a knot. Repeat for entire quilt top. When tying is complete, thread black ribbon through large-eyed needle and slip ribbon underneath cotton knot. Tie in a small neat knot. Repeat to cover each cotton tie.

figure 1

Log Cabin Quilts

The Log Cabin design is one of the most popular and versatile quilt patterns. It permits the utilization of a large variety of small strips of fabric arranged on horizontal and vertical planes. Half of the block is made of light and the other half of dark valued fabrics, working out from the red square at the centre meant to signify the hearth. Another technique, more commonly seen in wool quilts in the 19th century, was to fold the strips called "logs" one over the other, working out from the centre. This was assembled on a foundation and generally tied, as quilting was difficult through the layers and thicknesses of wool fabrics. There are several explanations for the origin of this very graphic design. The Royal Ontario Museum in Toronto has an exhibit of a mummified cat dated 30 BC to 100 AD whose wrappings and colours are similar to the log cabin design. Quilters on England's Isle of Man take credit for the design, meant to signify their plowed fields; half the furrows in sun, half in shade. In Ireland the design is called the Canadian or Loghouse quilt patchwork. Possibly the pattern was sent there from Canada by newly immigrated relatives.

The Sunshine and Shadows Log Cabin shows the arrangement of lights and darks and in its unfinished state allows us to see the method used to machine piece using assorted cotton squares for the foundation. At the beginning of the 20th century, quilters were limited to cotton, silk, and wool fabrics for their Log Cabin quilts. After the 1920s, rayon, the new synthetic, was often used to achieve the desired design effects of light and dark. Variations of the Log Cabin design are employed by contemporary quilters to create

Opposite: Incomplete Sunshine and Shadows quilt

dramatic visual pieces using the vast range of colours available in fabrics today.

The traditional "logs" block is built by sewing clockwise around the center square. The Courthouse Steps variation requires that you build two sides in pairs, on opposite sides of the centre square. The costumed ladies getting a hand-quilting lesson from Diane on a Pineapple variation Log Cabin design are at Kings Landing Historical Settlement on the Saint John River near Fredericton, NB. The

Satin Log Cabin pieced by Karen's great-grandmother, Christina Patterson of Five Islands, NS

textile curator made the quilt top the previous winter, reproducing an example in the collection of more than 200 quilts.

This picture of Diane's grandmother, Daisy Swan MacLeod, in front of a real Canadian log cabin was taken on her extended honeymoon in Alberta in 1913.

Pineapple Log Cabin, block size 11" (28 cm)

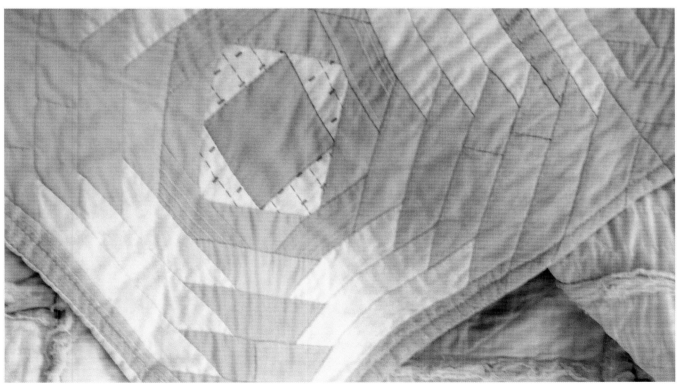

Log Canada Quilt

This patriotic design is based on a traditional Log Cabin "Courthouse Steps" pattern, with a maple leaf machine-appliquéd in each block centre. The gently scalloped edge adds a bit of movement to the flags. Sewing with strips makes this project go together quickly.

Cutting Instructions

From solid white, cut 35, 4-1/2" squares for the centres.

From solid red, cut 8, 1-1/2" strips for the first row of logs.

Cut **white-on-white and red prints** into 1-1/2" x WOF strips for logs. You will need a total of 200 strips.

From solid red, cut 8 WOF strips each 6-1/2" wide for outside border. Seam together in pairs along short ends to make four long border sections. Set aside.

Following manufacturer's instructions, apply fusible web to the back of 0.5 m (1/2 yard) of solid red. Using pattern supplied, cut out 35 maple leaf shapes. Set aside.

Materials
45" (115 cm) cotton

- 0.7 m (3/4 yard) solid white for centres
- 2.5 m (2-3/4 yard) solid red (first logs, maple leaf appliqués and outside border)
- 1 m (1-1/4 yard) each of 4 different white-on-white prints
- 1 m (1-1/4 yard) each of 4 different red prints
- 200 x 260 cm (78" x 102") batting
- 200 x 260 cm (78" x 102") backing
- 0.5 m (5/8 yard) fusible web
- 0.5 m (5/8 yard) tearaway fabric stabilizer
- 10 m (12 yards) bias binding or 0.5 m (5/8 yard) fabric to make binding
- Water soluble marker
- sewing and quilting thread to match

Finished size: 72" x 96"
Finished block size: 12"
Number of blocks total: 35

Note: Logs are 1"(cut 1-1/2") added to a 4" (cut 4-1/2") centre. All strips are cut WOF.

Directions

Sew 1-1/2" red strips (logs) to two sides of each white centre. (figure 1)

Trim ends even with white centre. Sew white logs to top and bottom. (figure 2)

Trim ends even with edge of block.

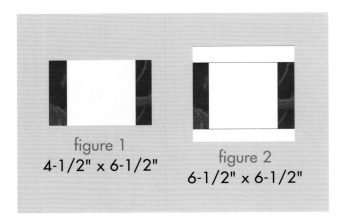

figure 1
4-1/2" x 6-1/2"

figure 2
6-1/2" x 6-1/2"

Continue adding logs in the same sequence (figures 3–8), trimming strips even with the end of the block after each addition. Press all seams away from centre. Blocks measure 12-1/2" square.

Remove paper backing from fusible web and fuse a maple leaf in the centre of each block. With tearaway stabilizer underneath the block and red thread in top of machine, work a narrow close zigzag around the leaf. Carefully remove stabilizer; tie and clip thread ends.

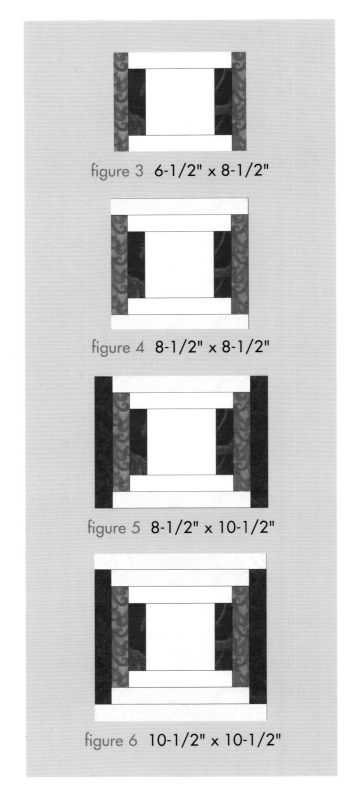

figure 3   6-1/2" x 8-1/2"

figure 4   8-1/2" x 8-1/2"

figure 5   8-1/2" x 10-1/2"

figure 6   10-1/2" x 10-1/2"

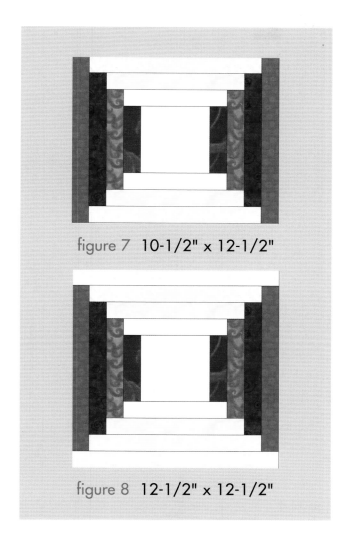

figure 7 10-1/2" x 12-1/2"

figure 8 12-1/2" x 12-1/2"

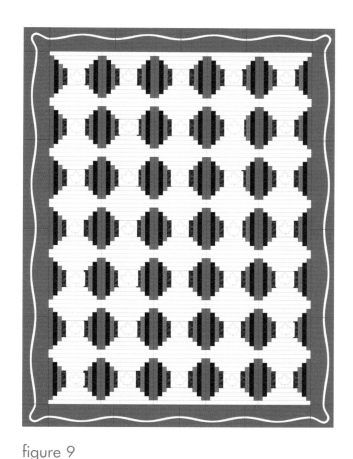

figure 9

Arrange blocks as shown, 5 blocks across and 7 down; sew together in rows, then sew rows together. (figure 9) Measure your quilt top across the centres, as in General Directions, and adjust the length of your borders accordingly. If your seam allowances have been exactly 1/4" your pieced top should

measure 60-1/2" x 84-1/2". Trim two red border strips to 84-1/2" or to the measurement of your pieced top through the centre and sew to sides of quilt, matching centre seam in the border to the centre of the quilt edge. Press seams toward border.

Trim two remaining borders to 96-1/2" or to your measurement across the centre and sew to top and bottom of quilt, centering border seam.

In outside border, trace around scallop shape provided, with water-soluble marker. Layer top, batting and backing. Baste layers together; hand or machine quilt as desired. Sample shown has a wreath of maple leaves quilted in the white section of logs, and a vine of maple leaves echoing the shape of the outside scalloped edge. When quilting is complete, stitch along scalloped edge through all layers and trim just outside stitched line. Bind edges.

This edge lines up with centre of white in blocks

Flip on this line for scallop repeat along length of border

Scallop Section B

Scallop border template: Place on border and trace using water-soluble marker. Section A is used at each corner. Section B is placed below Section A and flipped on the line marked along the length of the border.

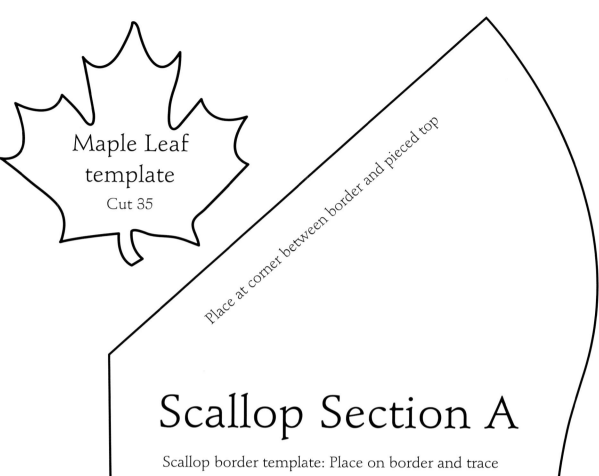

Maple Leaf template

Cut 35

Place at corner between border and pieced top

Scallop Section A

Scallop border template: Place on border and trace using water-soluble marker. Section A is used at each corner. Section B is placed below Section A and flipped on the line marked along the length of the border.

enlarge 115%

this piece only to measure

6-1/8" wide at bottom edge and 10-5/8" high

This edge lines up with centre of red in blocks

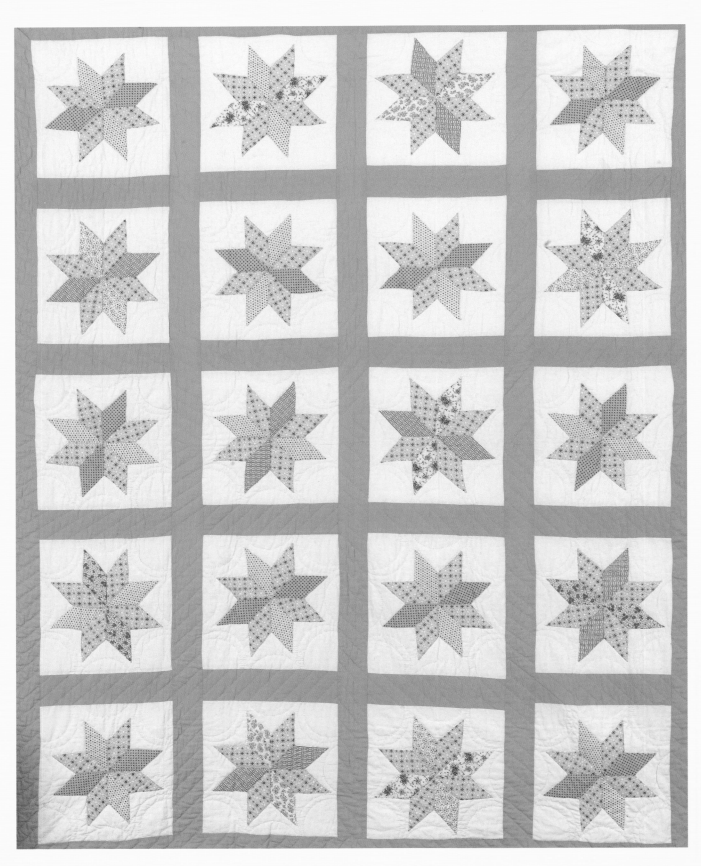

Le Moyne Star, 66" x 84" (168 x 213 cm)

46

Star Design Quilts

Stars, the oldest of designs occurring in the heavens, were a favoured subject of quilters for centuries. The Mi'kmaq use an eight-pointed star as one of their signature symbols. Star designs are found in hundreds of quilts in both block and overall format. The large variety of star designs go from easy to difficult, depending on the shape and number of points in the star. A test of a quilter's level of workmanship was to accurately piece a Bethlehem or Lone Star quilt so it would lie flat. The Six-pointed Radiant Star (below) made from hundreds of diamonds is unusual, as it does not have the customary eight points. The maker must have drafted this design herself. Shapes such as half-square or quarter-square triangles can be manipulated to give the effect of stars.

Using her Singer Featherweight sewing machine Jenny Macleod pieced yellow and green diamonds to make eight-pointed LeMoyne Stars and hand-appliquéd them with an invisible stitch onto bleached sugar bag blocks. The yard goods were obtained from her husband's general store in the village of River John, NS, in the 1950s. She always used white for the lining or backing of quilts (shown opposite). Diane's step-grandmother loved to hand quilt and like many rural women passed much of the winter at her quilting frame, which was set up in the dining room after Christmas. When asked a number of years ago if she still quilted, her reply was "of course in the winter." She preferred the process of quilting and simply did appliqué and machine piecing to get something to hand quilt. Others who preferred the piecing or appliqué process ended up with many unquilted tops, which we still find in trunks and closets. In the 21st century individuals using Long Arm Quilting machines finish these tops for a fee.

Six-pointed Star, c.1955, 71" x 87" (180 x 221 cm)

Star Kitchen Set

Dress up your kitchen with this co-ordinating set, including window valance, placemats, potholder and table runner. The Clay's Choice Stars are constructed with easy-to-make half-square triangles (HST).

Cutting Instructions

From tan print, cut 6, 2-1/4" strips x WOF and set aside for binding.

Cutting Instructions for 8" Clay's Choice Blocks: Enough for 10 blocks

From tan print, cut 3, 3" strips x WOF; recut into 40, 3" squares.

From red print, cut 2, 3" strips x WOF; recut into 20, 3" squares.

From red print, cut 3, 2-1/2" strip x WOF; recut into 40, 2-1/2" squares.

From cream print, cut 2, 3" strips x WOF; recut into 20, 3" squares.

From cream print, cut 3, 2-1/2" strips x WOF; recut into 40, 2-1/2" squares.

Cutting Instructions for 4" Clay's Choice Blocks: Enough for 3 blocks

From tan print, cut 1, 2" strip x WOF; recut into 12, 2" squares.

Materials
45" (115 cm) cotton

(to make valance, two placemats, runner and potholder. See page 51 for material needed for bottom curtain)

- 0.8 m (7/8 yard) cream print
- 1 m (1 yard) red print
- 1.5 m (1-2/3 yards) tan print
- 1 m (1 yard) batting (thin cotton recommended)
- 1 m (1 yard) backing
- 1 m (1 yard) lining for valance (may be matching print or plain cotton)
- sewing thread to match
- one 2 cm (3/4") plastic ring (for hanging potholder)
- 7 m (7-7/8 yards) binding for set or 1 m (1 yard) fabric to make binding

Finished block sizes: 8"; 4"
Number of blocks required for set:
10, 8" blocks
3, 4" blocks
Finished valance: 57" x 17"
Finished potholder: 8"
Finished runner: 42" x 18"
Finished placemat: 17-3/4" x 11-3/4"

From red print, cut 1, 2" strip x WOF; recut into 6, 2" squares.

From cream print, cut 1, 2" strip x WOF; recut into 6, 2" squares.

From red print, cut 1, 1-1/2" x WOF strip; recut into 12, 1-1/2" squares.

From cream print, cut 1, 1-1/2" x WOF strip; recut into 12, 1-1/2" squares.

Directions

Directions are given first for sewing the Clay's Choice block. Instructions for sewing individual projects are given separately under each heading.

Directions for 8" block: Refer to General Directions for making HST.

Place 20 cream 3" squares on top of 20 tan 3" squares to make 40 HST. Trim to 2-1/2". (figure 1)

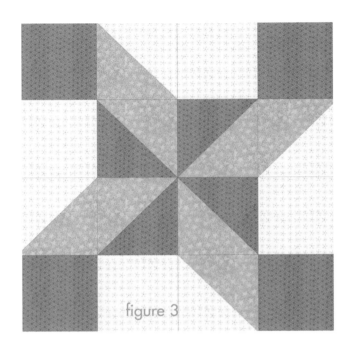

figure 3

figure 1

figure 2

Place 20 tan 3" squares on top of 20 red 3" squares to make 40 HSTs. (figure 2) Trim all HSTs to 2 1/2".

Arrange squares using the 2-1/2" plain red and cream squares. Sew together in rows then join rows. Your block will measure 8-1/2". (figure 3) Make 10 blocks.

Directions for 4" block:

Proceed as for 8" Clay's Choice blocks, using 2" squares for HST blocks. Trim these to 1-1/2". Arrange blocks using 1-1/2" plain red and cream squares. Your block will measure 4-1/2". Make 3 blocks.

figure 4

To Make the Valance

You will need 5, 8" blocks.

From tan print, cut 1, 12-1/2" square. Cut in quarters diagonally to form 4 triangles. These are used between blocks at the top of the valance.

From tan print, cut 1, 6-1/2"square. Cut in half diagonally to form 2 triangles. These are used at the blocks' ends.

From tan print, cut 2, 6-1/2" strips x WOF. Seam together on short ends to make one long piece. To centre the joining seam, measure 28-3/4" in each direction from this seam and mark. Trim on marks, so that your strip now measures 6-1/2" x 57-1/2", and your joining seam is centred in the strip. Sew strip to top of valance.

From lining fabric, cut 2 pieces 20" x WOF. Seam together on short end. Lay lining right side up and place pieced valance on top, right sides facing, matching centre seam in lining to centre point in valance. Pin edges and stitch around outside of valance, leaving an 8" opening on one short end to turn. Clip corners and into points, being careful not to cut into stitching. Turn right side out; press. Slipstitch opening closed using hand stitches. (figure 4)

To make top casing, turn the top edge 3" down to inside. This should just pass the seam line on the front of the valance. Pin. From the right side, stitch in the ditch of the seamline. Make another row of stitching 1" from top edge to form the ruffle. Curtain rod is inserted in the channel formed between these rows of stitching.

Note: Additional material required for bottom curtain is dependent on individual window measurements. Measure length and width of window. Purchase sufficient to add a 3" casing at top and a 4" hem to the length and to have double the width of the window.

To Make the Placemats

You will need 2, 8" blocks.

From tan print, cut 4, 6-1/2" squares. Cut 2 in half diagonally to form 4 triangles. Sew a triangle to each side of the block. Repeat for remaining squares.

From red print, cut 4, 1-1/2" strips x WOF.

From cream print, cut 2, 1-1/2" strips x WOF.

For end borders, seam strips together with the cream strip in between the two red strips. (figure 5) Press seam allowances to one side.

figure 5

Measure block and cut end border strip set this length (should be *approximately* 12"). Sew one strip set to each side of block. Press seams towards strips.

Layer, baste and quilt. Trim edges even and bind. (figure 6)

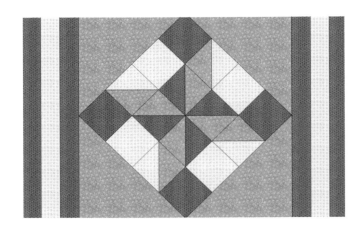

figure 6

To Make the Potholder

You will need 1, 8" block.

Piece 1, 8" block. A double layer of batting is used. Cut two squares of batting slightly larger than your block and stack one on top of the other. Cut 10" square of backing fabric and layer top, batting and backing. Baste and quilt. Trim edges even, bind. (figure 7) Sew plastic ring to one corner with hand stitches.

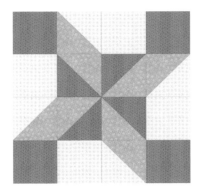

figure 7

To Make the Runner

You will need 2, 8" and 3, 4" blocks.

From tan print, cut 4, 6-1/2" squares. Cut each in half diagonally to form 2 triangles. Sew 1 triangle to each side of a pieced 8" block. Block measures 11-7/8".

From tan print, cut 6, 4-1/2" squares. Sew one to each end of 4" block. (figure 8, right) Sew one small block unit in between two 8" block units and one at each end.

From red print, cut 6 strips 1-1/2" x WOF.

From cream print, cut 3, 1-1/2" strips x WOF.

Sew 2 reds and a cream strip together, with the cream strip in between two red strips.

Repeat for remaining strips for a total of 3 strips sets. Cut one strip set in half lengthwise, and use these two shorter strip sets for the ends. Sew borders to placemat beginning and ending stitching 1/4" from ends, leaving ends of strips hanging free. Mitre corners. Layer, baste, and quilt. Trim edges even and bind. (figure 9, below)

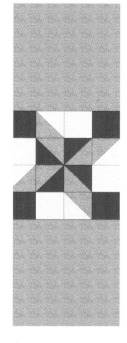

figure 8

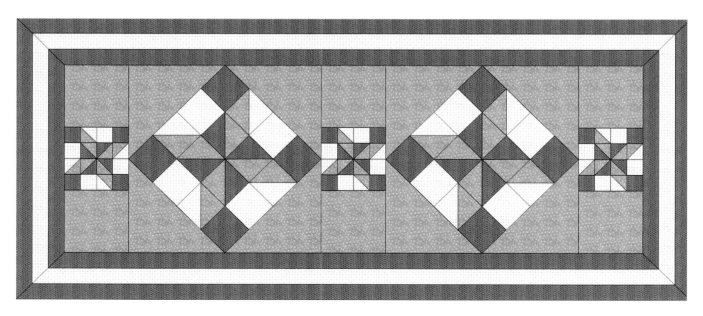

figure 9

Ohio Star Baby Set

This crib quilt and pillow feature Ohio Star blocks set on the diagonal with light-coloured sashing strips separating the blocks and triple plain, mitred borders. Faces are randomly machine stitched on several of the stars. If you like, add a small pocket on the back of the pillow to make a Tooth Fairy pillow.

Cutting Instructions

From blue print, cut 6, 3-1/4" x WOF strips; recut into 72, 3-1/4" squares.

From yellow print, cut 6, 3-1/4" x WOF strips; recut into 72, 3-1/4" squares.

From blue print, cut 4, 2-1/2" x WOF strips; recut into 54, 2-1/2" squares.

From yellow print, cut 3, 2-1/2" x WOF strips; recut into 36, 2-1/2" squares.

From blue print, cut 2, 5-1/8" squares; cut each in half diagonally to give 4 triangles. These are your corner triangles.

From blue print, cut 3, 9-3/4" squares; cut each in quarters diagonally to form 12 triangles. You will need 10 of these triangles in the outer border, 2 are discarded. These are your side triangles.

From white print, cut 4, 1-1/2" x WOF strips; recut into 24, 1-1/2" x 6-1/2" pieces for sashing strips between blocks.

From white print, cut 6, 1-1/2" x WOF strips. These will be recut into shorter lengths later for the sashing strips between rows.

From yellow print, cut 8, 1-1/2" x WOF strips for first border.

From white print, cut 8, 2-1/2" x WOF strips for second border.

From blue print, cut 8, 3-1/2" x WOF strips for outside border.

Materials
45" (115 cm) wide cottons

- 2 m (2-1/2 yards) blue print
- 1.4 m (1-1/2 yards) yellow print
- 1 m (1-1/4 yard) white print
- 5 m (5-2/3 yards) bias binding or 0.5 m (1/2 yard) fabric to make binding
- 1.5 m (1-2/3 yards) backing
- 1.5 m (1-2/3 yards) batting
- 0.25 m (1/4 yard) tear away stabilizer
- sewing and quilting thread to match
- blue machine embroidery thread for facial features
- water-soluble marker to draw facial features

Finished size: 42-1/2" x 52-1/2"
Block size: 6"
Number of blocks: 18 (12 blue blocks, 6 yellow blocks)

Directions

Refer to General Directions on how to make Quick Quarter-square Triangles. Using the blue and yellow 3-1/4" squares, sew 72 Quarter-square Triangles. Trim each to 2-1/2" square. (figure 1)

Using the 2-1/2" plain squares, assemble blocks as shown. Piece 12 blocks as shown. (figure 2) Piece 6 blocks as shown. (figure 3) Your blocks should measure 6-1/2" unfinished at this point; trim to square up as necessary. Arrange blocks as shown (figure 4) and sew a white print 1-1/2" x 6-1/2" sashing strip

figure 1

figure 2

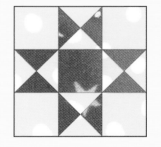

figure 3

in between the blocks in each row, as well as on either side of the end blocks.

Sew side triangles to the ends of each of the rows. Press seams away from block.

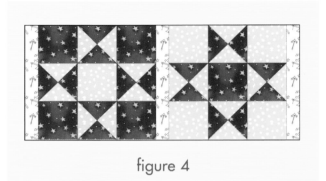

figure 4

You will need to measure your rows before cutting the 6, 1-1/2" sashing strips to length. If your seam allowance has been exactly 1/4" cut your strips to the following lengths. If your measurements are different, adjust as necessary.

From white print, cut 2, 1-1/2" x 8-1/2" pieces

From white print, cut 2, 1-1/2" x 22-1/2" pieces

From white print, cut 2, 1-1/2" x 36-1/2" pieces

From white print, cut 2, 1-1/2" x 42-1/2" pieces

Trim outside edges even as shown.
(figure 5)

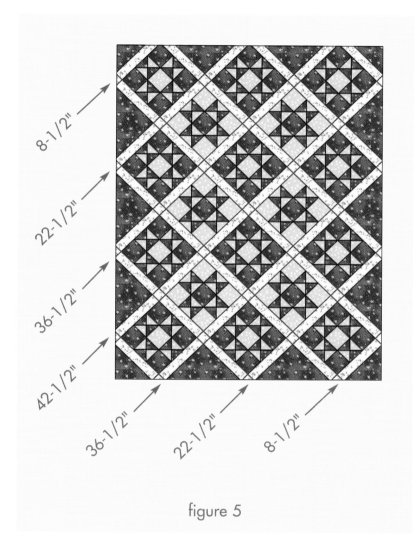

figure 5

strips. Repeat for the white print border strips and the blue print border strips. You will now have 4 long strips of each of three colours.

Lining up the centre seams, sew one yellow print and one white print strip together along the long edge. Press seam to one side. Repeat for remaining yellow print and white print strips. Sew one blue print border strip to the white print strip, lining up centre seams. Repeat for remaining border strips. You now have 4 long strips of yellow, white and blue.
(figure 6)

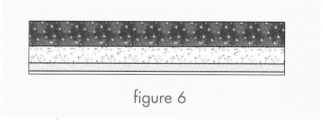

figure 6

To add borders:

Border strips are joined together first and then added as one piece to each side. Join the 4 yellow print border strips together in pairs along short ends to make 4 long yellow print

Measure quilt top in each direction as described in General Directions. Do not cut your borders to length, but mark the correct length on each border with a pin, measuring out from centre seam. You need extra to allow for the mitre at the corner.

Pin border to outside edges of pieced top, matching seam in border to the centre of the pieced top. Stitch, beginning and ending stitching 1/4" from each end. Mitre corners, press, and trim seam. (figure 7)

To make facial details:

Using water-soluble marker, draw face (figure 8) directly onto centre of star as shown in picture. With machine embroidery thread in top of machine and stabilizer underneath work, stitch using a narrow zigzag. Tie thread ends; clip. Carefully remove stabilizer. Refer to General Directions to layer, baste, quilt, and bind.

figure 8

figure 7

To Make the Pillow

From yellow print, cut 4, 4-1/4" squares and 1, 3-1/2" square.

From blue print, cut 4, 4-1/4" squares and 4, 3-1/2" squares.

From yellow print, cut 2, 5" strips x WOF.

Directions

Piece the block as for the quilt, making the quarter-square triangle units using the 4-1/4" squares. Trim to 3-1/2". Embroider the face. Place patchwork on top of batting square and machine quilt.

Sew the yellow print fabric strips for the ruffle together along both short ends to form a loop. Press in half widthwise, wrong sides together. Run a line of gathering stitches (i.e., the longest stitches your machine will sew) just inside the seam allowance on the raw edge. Divide the loop into quarters and mark with pins. Line up the pins to the centre of each side of the pieced block, and draw up the stitches to make the ruffle fit around the edge of the block. Pin in place and sew completely around the outside of the block.

Materials
45" (115 cm) wide cottons

Cotton fabric was included in quilt requirements given on page 55

Additionally you will need:
- 10" square of batting
- 225 grams (1/2 lb.) polyester fiberfill for stuffing
- 4" square of tearaway stabilizer
- 10" square of backing fabric.

Number of blocks used: 1
Finished size: 9" square plus ruffle
Block size: 9"

Place backing fabric right side down on top of the block and sew around the outside edge, leaving an opening to turn. Turn pillow right sides out, stuff with fiberfill and slipstitch opening closed with a few hand stitches.

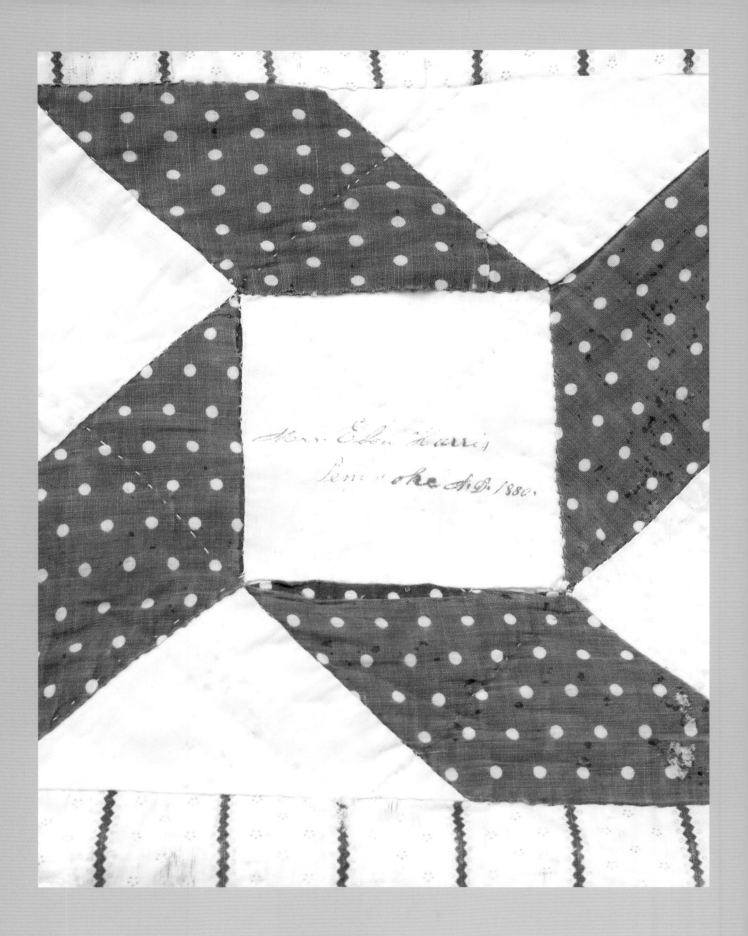

Signature Quilts

Signature quilts, also known as Friendship or Memory quilts, were made for a variety of reasons. Signatures were placed on quilts in one of two ways, either inked or embroidered. These quilts were often made as fundraisers or presentation gifts.

In 1880 the fashion of signing names on quilt blocks had spread to the Annapolis Valley of Nova Scotia. A few members of a Baptist church signed in ink the pictured Italian Tile block (shown opposite), as a presentation to their departing minister. It would have been difficult to date this quilt had it not been signed in ink, as polka dots, checks, stripes and plaids in fabric designs have always been common. This community custom of making and giving quilts to people before they departed due to marriage or changes in employment prevails in some areas to this day.

One hundred years ago most churches had women's sewing circles, Missionary societies, and/or fellowship groups which met during the week but never on a Sunday. In those days churches were the centre of community social activity. Women arranged their time and work schedules so they could attend these meetings which provided social stimulation and emotional support.

The Sutherland quilt made in the village of River John, NS, and dated 1909 has inked signatures all done in the same hand. Photographed in the cemetery beside the Presbyterian Church, this quilt has inked in a corner, "Quilted at the home of Mrs. McCann," the minister's wife.

Housed at the Fraser Cultural Centre, Tatamagouche, NS, is a red and white Delectable Mountain quilt dated 1901. Made by the Malagash Missionary Society, people paid to have their names embroidered on the triangles. The closer your name was to the middle the more it cost. Sometimes the finished quilt was also sold or raffled, thus generating more funds. Quilts of cotton

The Sutherland quilt, c.1909, 69" x 75" (175 x 190 cm)

Delectable Mountain quilt, dated 1901, from the Fraser Cultural Centre in Tatamagouche, NS. 66" x 66" (168 x 168 cm)

with a variety of signatures are commonly found throughout the Atlantic Provinces, generally in excellent condition, having been used for display rather than bedding.

Birthday Greetings, c.1939, a group quilt made near Sackville, NB, 74" x 80" (188 x 203 cm), block size 11.5" (29 cm)

met near Sackville, NB. Group-made quilts have been used as gifts to mark special occasions such as weddings or anniversaries. Throughout the years quilters have used the clothing of deceased relatives to make memorial quilts for those who have marked life's final passage.

Red Cross sewing circles and work groups made thousands of quilts destined for relief purposes in Canada and overseas during World Wars I & II.

One of Diane's quilts, a pink and white Ohio Star, has a repeating block format with names embroidered in various shades of pink and the words "Birthday Greetings 1939" in the central square. During an exhibit a few years ago a viewer recognized the names as those of her mother-in-law's bridge group who

Many of these quilts had a Red Cross label attached and, occasionally, a quilt is returned to the community of origin.

Signature from Delectable Mountain Quilt

Maple Leaf Signature Quilt

Signatures may be added before or after the quilt is constructed. If collecting signatures before sewing, you may wish to draw seam lines on the block with pencil to ensure that the signature does not extend into the seam line. There are a variety of permanent markers and pens on the market. Test first on the fabric you are using to ensure the ink does not bleed or smudge, and immerse it in water to make sure it will not fade when washed. Signatures may also be added after the quilt is constructed, as often happens at a family reunion so that the finished quilt may go home the same day with the lucky recipient.

Materials
45" (115 cm) wide cottons

- 2.5 m (2-3/4 yards) green print
- 1.25 m (1-1/3 yards) total of 26 assorted yellow, orange, red, gold and brown prints for leaves (each block requires two 3" squares, two 2-1/2" squares, two 1-1/4" squares and one 1-1/4" x 4" of the same print)
- 0.25 m (1/3 yard) brown
- 0.25 m (1/3 yard) ecru for signature part of leaf block
- 0.25 m (1/3 yard) each of 4 prints (red, yellow, gold and orange) for outer border
- 155 x 175 cm (61" x 69") batting
- 3.4 m (3-3/4 yards) backing (115 cm wide seamed for width)
- 6.5 m (7-1/4 yards) bias binding or 0.5 (5/8 yard) of fabric to make binding
- Permanent fine point markers or laundry pens suitable for writing on fabric
- Sewing and quilting thread to match

Finished size: 56" x 62"
Number of Maple Leaf Album blocks: 26
Finished Maple Leaf block size: 6"
Finished Centre Tree block size: 24" x 30"

Cutting Instructions

For Maple Leaf Album Blocks:

From green, cut 26, 6-1/2" squares.

From green, cut 52, 2-1/2" squares (26 are for

the stems, 26 are for plain units).

For Maple Leaf block:

From ecru, cut 26, 2-1/2" squares (for signature units).

From each print, cut 2, 2-1/2" squares per block (for a total of 52 for the quilt).

From each print, cut 2, 3" squares per block (for a total of 52 for the quilt).

From each print, cut 2, 1-1/4"squares (corners for the signature unit) for a total of 52.

From each print, cut 1, 1-1/4" x 4" piece (stems) per block, for a total of 26 stems.

From green print, cut 52, 3" squares (you will use 2 squares per block).

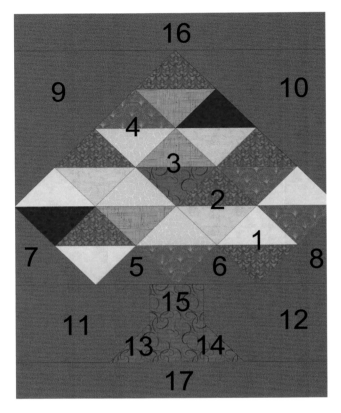

figure 1

For Outer Borders:

From red, cut 2, 4-1/2" wide pieces x WOF. Seam together on short ends.

From yellow, cut 2, 4-1/2" wide pieces x WOF. Seam together on short ends.

From gold, cut 2, 4-1/2" wide pieces x WOF. Seam together on short ends.

From orange, cut 2, 4-1/2" wide pieces x WOF. Seam together on short ends.

For Tree Block:

From green, cut 2, 24-1/2" x 3-1/2" pieces for top and bottom borders #16 and #17. (figure 1)

From green, cut 1, 13" square. Cut in half diagonally to give 2 triangles. These are #9 and #10. (figure 1)

Cut 1, 7" green square. Cut in half diagonally to give 2 triangles. These are #7 and #8. (figure 1)

From green, cut 2, 6-1/2" x 10-1/2" rectangles. These are #11 and #12. (figure 1)

From green, cut 1, 5" square. Cut in half diagonally to give 2 triangles. These are #5 and #6. (figure 1)

From brown, cut 2, 4" squares. These are for the triangles at the base of the trunk, #13 and #14. (figure 1)

From brown, cut 1, 4-1/2" x 6-1/2" rectangle for the tree trunk, #15. (figure 1)

For the leaves: Cut 8 squares of assorted prints, each 5-1/4" square.

Sewing Directions

For Tree Block:

Make half-square triangle blocks using 8, 5-1/4" squares. Trim to 4-3/4" square. You need 13 HST for the tree; discard the extras. Lay out leaves in rows as shown. Sew green triangles #5 and #6 (figure 1) to the end of rows 1 and 2. Join rows in order from 1 to 4. Add green #7 and #8 triangles and green #9 and #10 triangles. (figure 1)

Piece the trunk section by drawing a line diagonally from corner to corner on a brown

4" square. Place this square on a corner of green #11 rectangle and stitch on drawn line. Trim seam allowance 1/4" past stitching. Repeat for section 12, making sure you are sewing the #14 square on the opposite corner from the #11-13 unit. Use picture as a guide. Sew the brown #15 trunk section between the #11 and #12 sections. Sew this pieced trunk section to bottom of leaves section. Sew green 24-1/2" x 3-1/2" piece to top and bottom of this block, which now measures 24-1/2" x 30-1/2".

To make the Maple Leaf Album blocks

Make half-square triangle blocks using two, 3-1/4" squares of print and 2, 3-1/4" squares of green. This will yield 4 HST blocks. (See General Directions.) Trim to 2-1/2". For the stem block cut 2-1/2" green square in half diagonally to form 2 triangles. Centre and sew 1-1/4" x 4" print strip between cut triangles. Trim block to 2-1/2" square.

Draw a line diagonally on each of the two print 1-1/2" squares. Place each square on opposite corners of ecru 2-1/2" square. Sew on line. Trim seam allowance to 1/4" past stitching; repeat for opposite corner. Press flat.

Assemble block as shown. (figure 2) Block measures 6-1/2". Repeat for a total of 26 Maple Leaf Album blocks. Arrange blocks as shown (figure 3), alternating maple leaf blocks with plain 6-1/2" green blocks. Sew side leaf units on first, then top and bottom units. Press seams away from centre block. (figure 4)

Measure quilt for borders and sew to top as shown below. (figure 5) Layer, baste, and quilt as desired. Trim edges even and bind.

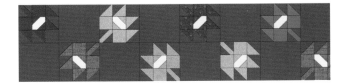

figure 3

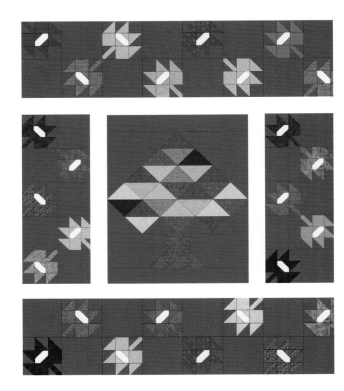

figure 4

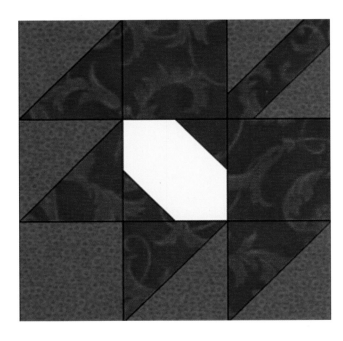

figure 2

figure 5

Crazy Quilts
Recycling something for nothing

Crazy Quilts were a fad associated with the material abundance and glitz of the Victorian era. They were hand-pieced from various shades of irregular-shaped pieces of sewing scraps sewn to foundation blocks of cheaper cotton. In a true Crazy Quilt every seam is covered with a variety of elaborate stitches using colourful threads made of silk, metallic or pearle cotton. Fans, a popular design motif in Victorian households, were sometimes pieced from velvet or ribbons. Good luck designs such as the spider web and horseshoe were painted or embroidered on the pieces. It is not uncommon to find tobacco silks and commemorative ribbons included in the blocks. The thickness and detailing on the surface meant that those finished were often tied or tufted rather than quilted. Most crazy quilts contain at least one date and often initials, occasionally in a fancy monogram of the maker, making this one of the few times when quilters were not anonymous.

When silk was unavailable cottons and wools were used. Women from all economic levels did crazy work, as it was very stylish to be working on a crazy patch. Even sea captains' wives worked on crazy patch blocks while accompanying husbands on long voyages. Those that were completed display the most elaborate of edge finishes from braided tassels, fabric fringes, and lace to satin ribbons. Many are still being discovered in pristine unused condition since these projects

Tobacco silks commonly found in crazy quilts

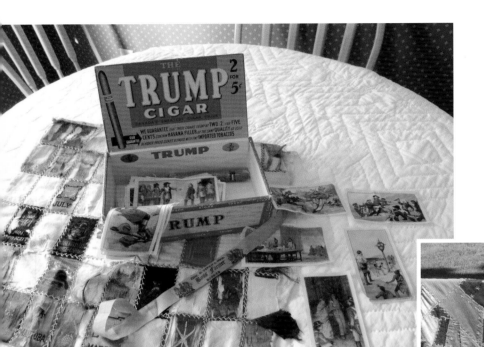

Left: Tobacco silks stitched into a pillow top

Bottom: Wool Crazy Quilt, 69" x 72" (175 x 183 cm)

Opposite page: Silk Crazy Quilt, c.1890

were abandoned after Queen Victoria's death. Thousands were made and a great many have survived.

In her diaries L.M. Montgomery reminisces about the crazy quilt she made between 1886 and 1890, spending countless hours covering the fabrics with intricate stitches, some of which she invented. When she re-found the quilt in 1920, she found it hideous and wondered why she had wasted $1 purchasing mail order dressmakers' cuttings from an American silk firm. However, in her reminiscences, she stated, "I had the joy of the making and that was the essence of heaven."

The Crazy Quilt pictured on page 70 was made by Nova Scotian Jessie McIntosh, who worked in Boston where her portrait was taken. She brought the quilt back to Bayhead in northern Nova Scotia when she married in 1900. It was used for many years as a cover for a trunk in the MacLennan farmhouse. Despite its worn condition her granddaughter treasures it.

52" x 62" (132 x 157 cm)

French Silk Quilt

This sumptuous lap quilt is made from recycled silk blouses purchased at a favourite Maritime second-hand clothing store. The silk scraps are sewn onto non-removable fabric foundations and embellished with the labels and buttons from the garments, as well as a bit of decorative machine stitching. A sashing of black satin is used to set the blocks together. If your machine does only straight stitch, try adding lace embellishments or specialty thread to add some interest. Anything goes — it's a crazy quilt!

Cutting Instructions

From foundation fabric, cut 20, 8-1/2" squares. From silk cut small pieces as required ranging from 2" to 6" in various shapes: squares, rectangles, diamonds, triangles. Include interesting features from the garment construction such as collars or cuffs. Remove buttons, labels and any trim which you wish to reuse from the blouses.

From black satin, cut 4, 2-1/2" wide strips; recut into 15, 2-1/2" x 8-1/2" sashing strips between blocks and 4, 2-1/2" x 38-1/2" pieces for sashing strips between rows.

From black satin, cut 8, 4-1/2" pieces x WOF for outer borders. Seam together in pairs on short ends to make 4 long pieces.

Materials
45" (115 cm) wide fabrics

- 1.5 m (1-2/3 yards) lightweight fabric for foundation (such as non-fusible woven interfacing or cotton broadcloth)
- 1.5 m (1-2/3 yards) black satin
- Recycled silk (blouses, skirts) yielding enough fabric to equal approximately 1.5 m (1-2/3 yards)
- Labels, buttons, trim for embellishments
- 3.5 m (3-7/8 yards) fabric for backing
- 6 m (6-3/4 yards) gold braid
- 4 gold tassels
- Specialty threads for machine embroidery, such as silk, metallic, rayon and cotton

Finished size: 46" x 56"
Block size: 8"
Number of blocks used: 20

How to do Crazy Patch

As the name implies, the patchwork is done in no set pattern. Odd-shaped fabric pieces are randomly applied to cover the foundation. (figure 1) Place the first piece of silk right side up near the centre of the foundation. Place another piece right side down on top of this and seam the two pieces together along one side. (figure 2) Trim seam allowance to 1/4". Flip the second piece to the back and press. (figure 3) Continue adding pieces of fabric in this manner until the foundation is completely covered. Trim the patchwork even with the edges of the foundation square. Make 20 blocks. Using specialty threads cover each seam with a zigzag or decorative stitch. Machine stitch labels in place, as well as any trim or braid.

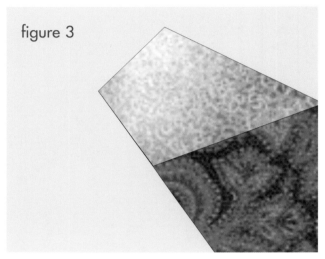

figure 2

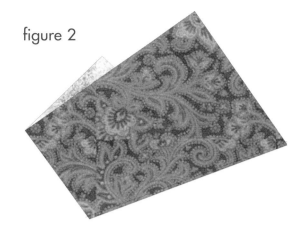

figure 3

Sew 2-1/2" x 8-1/2" black sashing strips to the ends of blocks and arrange in rows 4 blocks across. (figure 4)

Arrange rows as shown. (figure 5) Press seams away from blocks. Add 2-1/2" x 38-1/2"

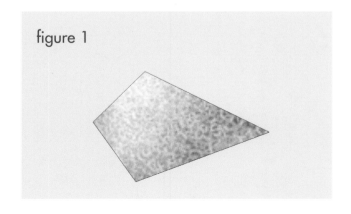

figure 1

figure 4

sashing strips between rows. Press.
Measure quilt top for borders. Add borders,
pressing seams away from centre. (figure 6)

Add backing fabric; baste. Work a decorative
stitch around the outside of
each block and through the
centre of the sashing strips
to secure the backing. Trim
edges even. Clean finish
edges of quilt by zigzagging
or serging. Fold braid in half
over outside edge and
topstitch in place with
matching thread,
overlapping ends. Stitch
tassels to each corner with
a few hand stitches. Add
buttons, etc., by hand.

figure 5

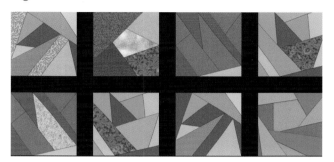

figure 6

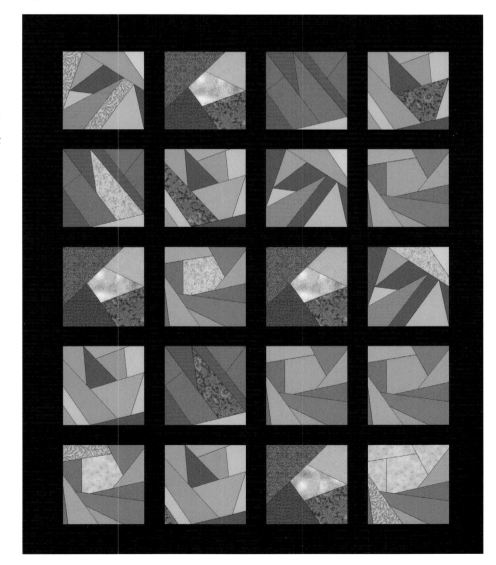

Little Red Hen Quilt

"Who will help me?" asked the little red hen.
"Not I," grunted the pig from his muddy patch in
the garden. "Not I," quacked the duck from her
pond. "Not I," purred the cat from his place in
the sun. "Very well," said the little red hen.
"I shall make the bread myself."

In this quilt, blocks are laid out to create a star in the centre with chickens running every which way around the outside, much as in the story of the "Little Red Hen." Feedsacks are reproduced by means of an inkjet printer.

Cutting Instructions

From muslin, cut 2, 2-1/2" x 30-1/2" pieces.

From muslin, cut 2, 5-1/2" x 60-1/2" pieces.

From yellow, cut 2, 4-1/2" x 60-1/2" pieces along the length of fabric.

From yellow, cut 2, 4-1/2" x 40-1/2" pieces.

From red, for prairie point wings, cut 4, 4" x WOF strips; recut into 32, 4" squares.

From yellow, for combs, cut 1, 1-1/2" x WOF strip; recut into 32, 1-1/2" squares.

Materials
45" (115 cm) cottons

- 2.6 m (2-5/8 yards) muslin
- 1.6 m yellow (1-5/8 yards)
- 0.9 m red (1 yard)
- 0.25 m gold (1/4 yard)
- 135 cm x 185 cm (54" x 74") batting
- 3.5 m (3-7/8 yards) backing (pieced for width)
- Freezer paper
- Bubble Jet Set OR 7 purchased, pre-treated 8-1/2" x 11" fabric sheets for ink-jet printers
- 0.25 m (1/3 yard) fusible web for the appliquéd sunrise block
- 0.25 m (1/3 yard) tearaway fabric stabilizer
- 7 m (7-7/8 yards) binding or 0.5 (1/2 yard) fabric to make binding
- Yellow topstitching thread (for stitching chicken legs)
- 64 small, 1/8" black sequins or buttons (for chicken eyes)
- Sewing and quilting thread to match
- Ink jet printer/computer
- Pencil

Finished size: 48" x 68"
Finished Block Size: 6" in main part of quilt; 2 sunrise blocks 7" x 30"
Number of blocks: 8 Chicken A blocks; 16 Chicken B blocks; 4, 6" HST blocks; 4, 4" HST blocks; 2 Sunrise blocks

From muslin, cut 2, 7-1/2" x 30-1/2" pieces.

From muslin, cut 2, 7" x WOF strips; recut into 10, 7" squares.

From muslin, cut 2, 7-1/2" x WOF strips; recut into 8, 7-1/2" squares.

From red, cut 2, 7-1/2" x WOF strips; recut into 8, 7-1/2" squares.

From red, cut 2, 5" squares.

From muslin, cut 2, 5" squares.

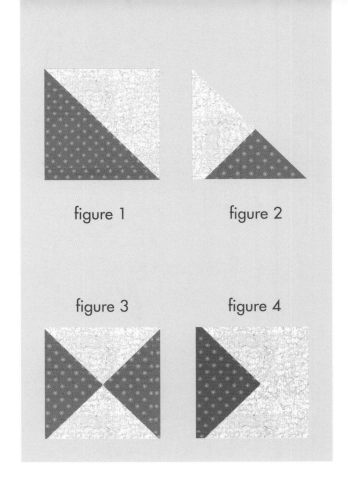

figure 1   figure 2

figure 3   figure 4

To make 6" half-square triangles (HST) see General Directions.

Place a 7" muslin square on top of a 7" red square to make HST blocks. Square up your block to 6-1/2". Repeat with second set of squares to yield 4 HST. (figure 1)
Repeat as per above using 5" red and muslin squares to make corner blocks for outer border. Square your blocks to measure 4-1/2". Make 4.

Cut 8 muslin and 8 red 7-1/2" squares diagonally corner to corner in each direction to form 4 triangles. Sew these red and muslin

triangles together in pairs. (figure 2)

Join 16 pairs to make 8 blocks. (figure 3) Square up to 6-1/2". This is Chicken Block A.
Cut 8, 7" muslin squares in half diagonally to form 2 triangles. Sew these muslin triangles to remaining red/white triangles to make 16 blocks like this. (figure 4) This is Chicken Block B.

To make Prairie Point wings

Fold the 32, 4" red squares in half diagonally,

and then in half diagonally again. Press flat. Centre these prairie points on top of the red triangles in both Chicken A and Chicken B blocks so that the points are aligned. Machine baste in place.

To make Prairie Point combs

Fold 32, 1-1/2" yellow squares in half diagonally, and then diagonally again, forming a small triangle. Press. In Chicken B block, place combs to the right of the prairie point wing, at the edge of the triangle, and baste in place. In Chicken Block A, alternate the combs so that they are on opposite ends of the chicken. By hand, stitch a black sequin on each block for the chicken's eye.

To make feedbags

You will need to scan the supplied feedbag graphic on page 85 (figure 10) into your computer, or take it to a print shop to have it photocopied onto treated fabric sheets. Pre-treated fabric sheets are widely available for purchase, or you can make your own.

Consult your printer manual for proper setting for printing on fabric. (figure 5)

To make your own printable fabric sheets

Follow directions on Bubble Jet Set or similar product to treat the fabric. After treating, cut fabric roughly into 8-3/4" x 11-1/2" pieces. Iron freezer paper to the back of the fabric and trim to 8-1/2" x 11", ensuring that edges are smooth for feeding into the printer. Print the block. Repeat to make 7 blocks. After printing, remove freezer paper from back of fabric and proceed as directed by

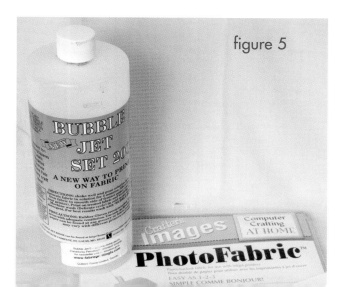

figure 5

manufacturer for setting the ink to dye.
(figure 6) If using purchased, pre-treated fabric
sheets, proceed as per manufacturer's
instructions and print graphic directly onto
fabric sheet. After printing, trim each feedsack
block to 6-1/2" square, making sure to centre
the design when trimming.

Lay out blocks as shown. Sew together in
rows; sew rows together. Chicken A blocks
form the center star design with Chicken B
blocks around the outside and large HST
blocks in corners. (figure 7) Sew 2-1/2" x 30-
1/2" muslin borders to top and bottom of
patchwork.

To make Sunrise block

Apply fusible web to back of yellow, gold,
and red fabric. Cut out shapes from
appropriate colours using templates supplied
(pages 84-85). Templates A, C, E, and G are
cut from yellow. Template D is cut from red.
Templates B and F are cut from gold.
Yellow centre E and red band D are both
placed on the fold of the fabric before cutting.

figure 6

Position pieces as shown (figure 8) on the 7-
1/2" x 30-1/2" muslin piece and fuse in place
using a hot iron. Place tearaway stabilizer
underneath work. Using yellow thread in top

figure 7

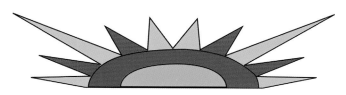

of machine, work a satin stitch (close zigzag) around all raw edges of fabric. Pull thread ends to back of work, tie and clip. Carefully remove tearaway. Repeat to make second block. Sew blocks to top and bottom of patchwork. Press seams toward plain border strip.

Sew 5-1/2" x 60-1/2" muslin borders to each side. Press seams toward border strip just added. Sew yellow 4-1/2" x 60-1/2" strips to each side of quilt. Sew one HST to both ends of one 4-1/2" x 40-1/2" yellow top/bottom border strip. Repeat for remaining strip. Sew borders to top and bottom of quilt. Press seams towards yellow borders.

To Stitch Chicken Legs

With tear-away stabilizer underneath work

figure 9

and yellow thread in top of machine, stitch 2, 1" legs on the underside of each chicken triangle. Add a black sequin to each chicken with hand stitches in the appropriate place for an eye.

Layer, baste and quilt as desired. When quilting is complete, trim edges even and bind. (figure 9)

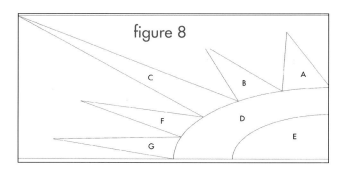

figure 8

Little Red Hen Sunrise Block templates

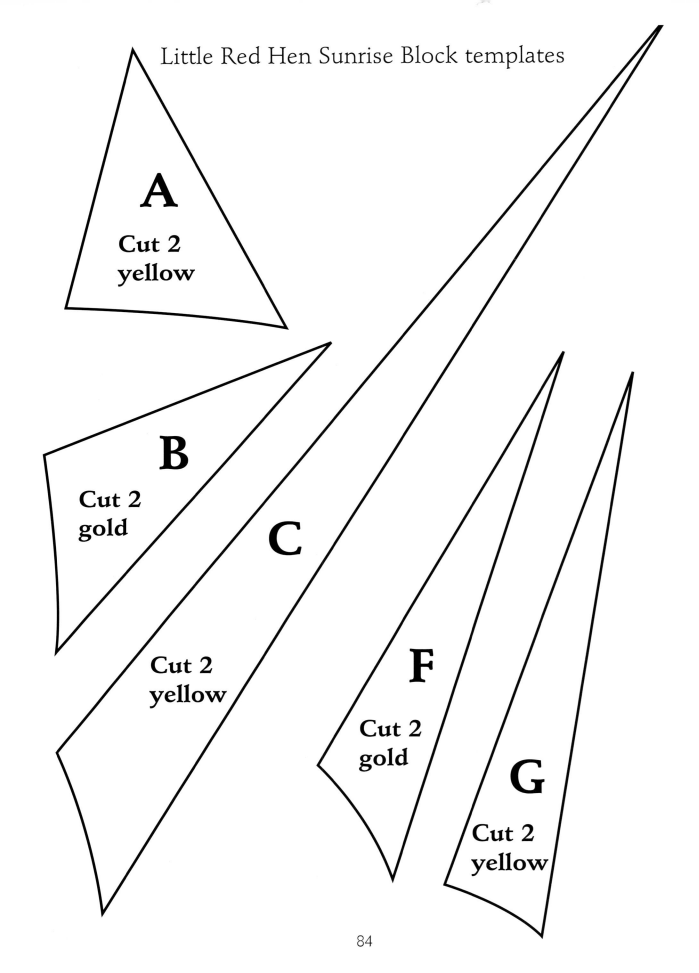

A

**Cut 2
yellow**

B

**Cut 2
gold**

C

**Cut 2
yellow**

F

**Cut 2
gold**

G

**Cut 2
yellow**

Little Red Hen Sunrise Block templates

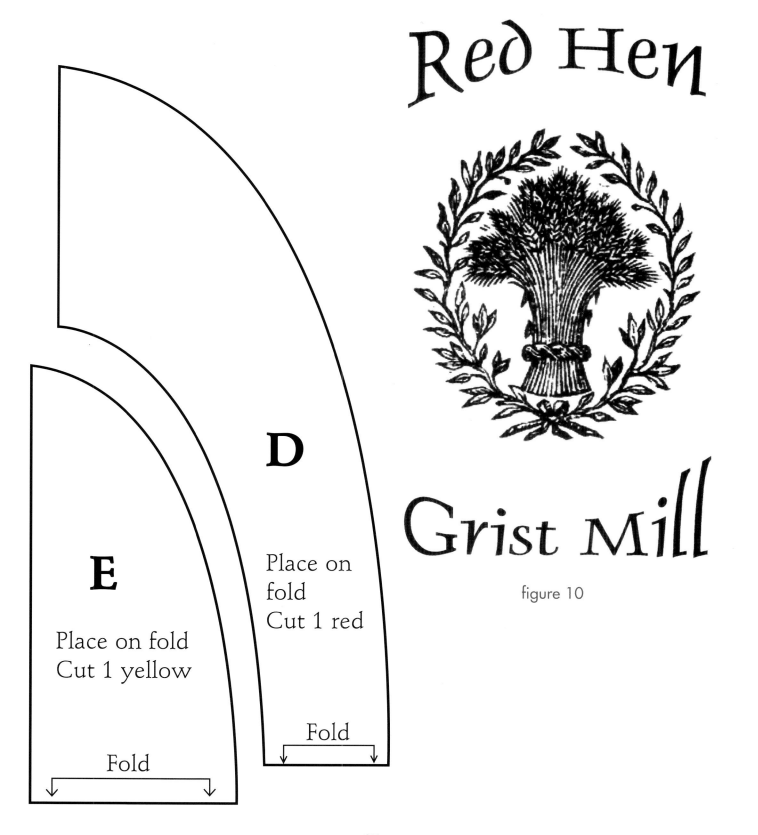

E

Place on fold
Cut 1 yellow

Fold

D

Place on
fold
Cut 1 red

Fold

Red Hen

Grist Mill

figure 10

Fans and Quilting
in the Great Depression

"Use it up, Wear it out, Make it do, or Do without" was the mantra of the 1930s. Housewives were encouraged to recycle and Home Economics sections of provincial governments distributed instructions for making quilts and recycling adult clothing into children's outfits. During most of the 20th century flour, sugar, animal feed and seed bags made of cotton were of a quality that was useful for making household items. The thrifty homemaker dyed these textiles to get a variety of colours. The fan design was often the one chosen to make quilts of these recycled textiles.

Pink and White Fan quilt, c. 1930, stitched by Karen's grandmother Myrtle Davis (pictured with her husband, Austen), 75" x 85" (190 x 216 cm)

One of the issues when making a quilt was acquiring the backing or lining to finish the quilt. The term "putting in a quilt" is used to explain the process of getting the 3 layers into a frame ready for quilting. During the depression it was often necessary to use pieced feed sacks for the backing, identified by the presence of square pieces rather than vertical strips. Three generations of families frequently lived under the same roof, so mother and daughter helped grandmother mark the quilt, using household objects such as cups, glasses and plates to create designs for quilting. They used lead pencil or chalk to get the designs on the quilt. All-over designs, such as radiating curved lines called the Baptist fan, were made using a pencil and string. Today it is possible to buy plastic templates of designs for hand quilting and cotton backing is made specifically for quilts in widths to accommodate king-sized beds.

For some people quilts are associated with negative feelings, especially poverty. Families who were poor and hungry during the depression used homemade quilts because they could not afford to buy blankets and even today looking at quilts can bring back bad memories. Invalids and people with contagious diseases, such as tuberculosis, made quilts to pass the time. The finished products were burned for fear of transmission of the disease. But quilting also brought families together. Many stories are told of sisters who lived in different communities getting together, often during the summer, to help each other finish quilts.

Opposite page: Fan quilt, "Snake Set", part of the "Quilts with a Story" exhibit, 2004, 75" x 85" (190 x 216 cm)
Right: Kite design quilt with feed sack backing, pieced in 1940 and quilted by Diane in 1995, 29" x 29" (74 x 74 cm)

Gram's Baptist Fans

1930s reproduction prints and cotton batting add to the old-fashioned charm of this quilt. The block has been designed in such a way as to allow it to be completely machine pieced. It has been machine quilted in an all over Baptist Fan pattern. To duplicate this, trace around a plate in concentric circles.

Cutting Instructions

(Templates, pages 92-93)

From assorted prints, cut 480, using fan blade template A.

From pink, cut 80, using centre quarter circle B template.

From pink, cut 80 on the fold of the fabric, using top band C template.

From eggshell, cut 80 on the fold of the fabric, using background template D.

From eggshell, cut 18, 6-1/2" squares for border triangles; cut each in half diagonally to make 36 triangles.

From assorted prints, cut 90 blades, using border fan template E.

Materials
45" (115 cm) cottons

- 4 m (4-1/2 yards) pink (this amount includes enough to make bias binding; if purchasing ready-made, you will need 13 m (14-3/4 yards) of bias binding
- 3.5 m (3-7/8 yards) eggshell (background)
- 6.5 m (7-1/4 yards) total of assorted prints (fan blades) (Fat Quarters give a nice assortment)
- 5 m (5-2/3 yards) backing fabric
- 208 x 250 cm batting (82" x 98")
- Sewing and quilting thread to match

Finished block size: 8"
Border blocks: 5-3/4"
Finished quilt size: 76" x 91-1/2"
Number of blocks required for quilt: 80
Number of blocks in border: 30

Directions

Join 6 assorted fan blades to make one unit. Make 80 fan blade units. (figure 1)

figure 1

Press to mark centre of pink quarter centre circles (figure 2) and match this mark to

figure 2

centre of shorter edge of pieced fan blade units, right sides together. (figure 3)

figure 3

Pin and sew. (figure 4) Press to mark centre of

figure 4

top band and match and pin to centre top of fan blades. (figure 5) Sew. (figure 6)

figure 5

figure 7

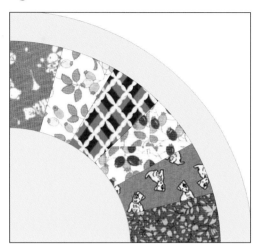

figure 6

figure 8

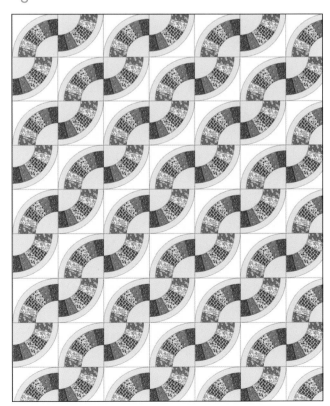

Press and mark centre of eggshell background and match to centre of top pink band. Pin and sew. Repeat for 80 fan blocks. (figure 7)

Lay out blocks in rows as shown (figure 8), 8 across and 10 down. Sew blocks together in rows, then join rows together.

To Make Borders

Piece border fans using 3 assorted prints to make one fan unit. Make 30 fan units. Join alternately with triangles, beginning and ending with a triangle. (Triangles are the 6-1/2" squares cut in half.) For 2 side borders, use 7 fans and 8 triangles. For the top and bottom borders, use 10 triangles and 9 fans. (figure 9) Sew borders to all sides of quilt.

figure 9

To make corner, sew two border fan sections together. Sew across end border triangles. Repeat for remaining 3 corners. (figure 10) Press top. Layer quilt, baste, quilt, and bind with bias binding.

figure 9

Gram's Fans Border Fan Blade template

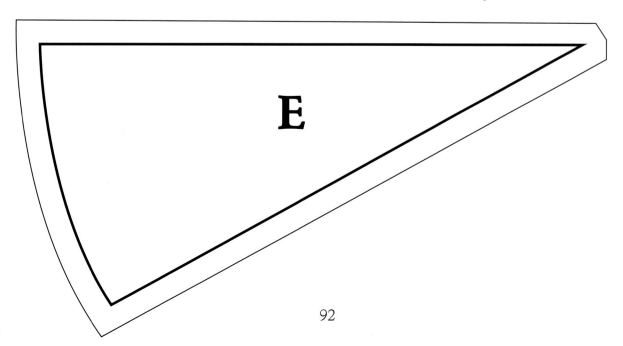

E

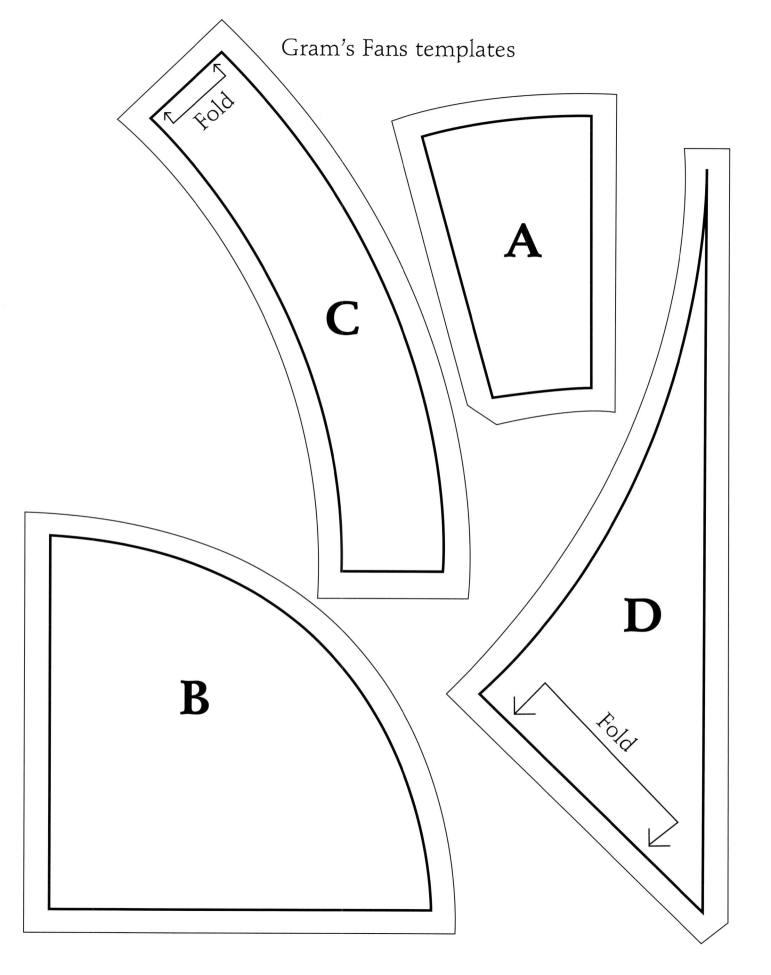

Gram's Fans templates

Fold

C

A

B

D

Fold

Mariner's Compass Quilts

The mariner's compass is associated with the sea and navigation; circular in shape, the design was used in quilts, but no 19th-century Mariner's Compass Quilts have been found in the Atlantic Provinces. A late 20th-century compass quilt made and quilted by hand was located in Nova Scotia. The compass pattern required exact cutting and piecing and today the accuracy is guaranteed by using the paper piecing technique.

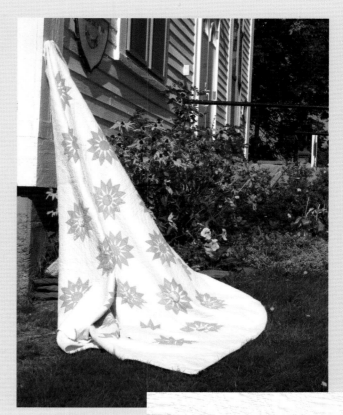

Weatherby Sunflower quilt, c.1885, 68" x 74" (172 x 188 cm), block size 10" (25 cm)

The Mariner's Compass design has points of various lengths, while the points on the Sunflower patterns are all the same size. Some of the finest hand quilting we see to this day was executed in the third quarter of the 19th century. The Russian sunflower has realistic brown centres with an elaborate appliquéd vine border, an unusual addition for a quilt from the Atlantic Provinces. The chromium yellow and white sunflower was made near Truro, NS, over a hundred years ago. It appears that the designs were hand-pieced and then set into the circles.

Above: Russian Sunflower quilt, possibly part of an 1856 wedding trousseau, c.1875, 78" x 84" (198 x 213 cm)

Opposite: Closeup of Mariner's Compass quilt, c.1975, 79" x 79" (200 x 200 cm), block size 18" (45.5 cm)

This quilt is believed to have been made by Martha Jane Weatherby in Belmont, NS, who was born around the time when the Dominion of Canada was created. It was taken to the prairies by the Weatherby grandchildren and returned to Nova Scotia in 1997 for a family reunion.

Sunflower Compass Placemats

Foundation piecing makes these sharp compass points a snap to sew. The centre circle is machine appliquéd with invisible nylon thread. Scalloped ends echo the circular design of the sunflower.

Cutting Instructions

From ecru background print, cut 8, 7-1/4" squares (you need 2 per placemat).

From ecru background print, cut 3, 3" strips x WOF (end borders on placemats).

From green print, cut 16 of Corner Block template (page 100).

Directions

Using patterns supplied (page 100), make 16 copies each of Section A and Section B foundations. You will need 4 of each section to complete one compass block. In the sample shown the colours are used as follows:

Section A:

Ecru background print: A1 and A3

Light Yellow: A2

Dark Gold Print: A4

Section B:

Ecru background print: B1 and B3

Dark Yellow: B2

Materials
45" (115 cm) cottons

(to make 4 placemats)

- 1 m (1-1/4 yards) ecru print (background)
- 0.25 m (1/3 yard) each of yellow, dark gold print, dark yellow & sunflower print
- 0.10 m (1/8 yard) brown print (sunflower centres)
- 0.5 m (5/8 yard) green print
- 1.3 m (1-1/2 yards) backing
- 1.3 m (1-1/2 yards) backing
- 6.4 m (7-1/4 yards) bias binding or 0.5 m of green fabric to make binding
- Sewing and quilting thread to match
- Invisible thread for appliqué
- Water-soluble marker

Finished size: 17-1/2" x 12-3/4"

Sunflower print: B4

Refer to General Directions for foundation piecing instructions. After blocks are trimmed,

figure 1

sew appropriate sections together.

Note: B4 looks as though it has an inset seam, but does not. It is this odd shape to accommodate the centre circle. Nothing special needs to be done for this seam; proceed as with the others.

When sections are all joined, press seams in one direction. Stitch a scant 1/4" around the outside edge of the block. Gently remove paper from back. (figure 1)

From brown print, cut compass centre using circle pattern provided. Turn under 1/4" seam allowance and press. Machine appliqué in place in centre of compass using invisible nylon thread and a narrow blind hem or zigzag stitch. (figure 2)

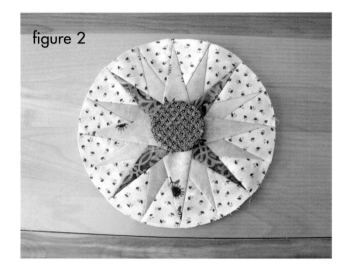

figure 2

Using 4 of the green print Block Corner sections, fold in half and press to mark centre. (figure 3)

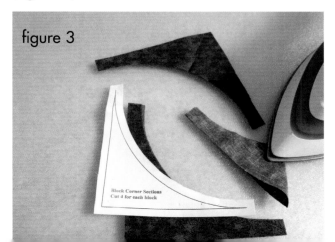

figure 3

Block Corner Sections
Cut 4 for each block

Right sides together, sew 2 sections together along one short end. Repeat for remaining two sections. Open each up and place one section on top of the other, right sides together. Sew remaining seams to join the unit into a circle. Press seam allowances open. Lay this pieced green circle section on top of the compass unit, right sides together, and match the seams in the circle unit to each large point on the compass (the Sunflower print used in B4). (figure 4) Pin around the compass. Stitch. Press seams away from centre of compass.

figure 5

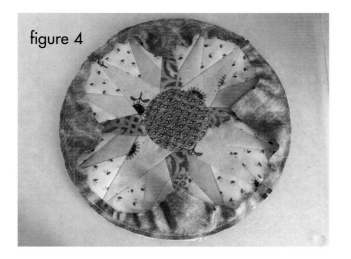

figure 4

Cut 2, 7-1/4" ecru background squares in half diagonally to make 4 triangles and sew 2 triangles to opposite sides of the compass.

Press seam allowance away from block. Repeat for top and bottom of block. Block now measures 13-1/8" square. If your block is a different size you will need to adjust the length of the end borders. Using the 3" x WOF strips, cut into 8, 13-1/8" lengths or the size of your block. You will use 2 pieces per placemat. Sew a strip to opposite sides of each block. Press seam allowance away from mat.

Lay scallop template in place on end borders (it will end at the centre) and trace using water-soluble marker. Flip template end-to-end at centre of border and continue tracing the length of the border. Stitch along this line. (figure 5) Layer top, batting and backing. Pin baste and quilt as desired. When quilting is complete, trim scallop on end just outside stitching. Trim edges even. Bind.

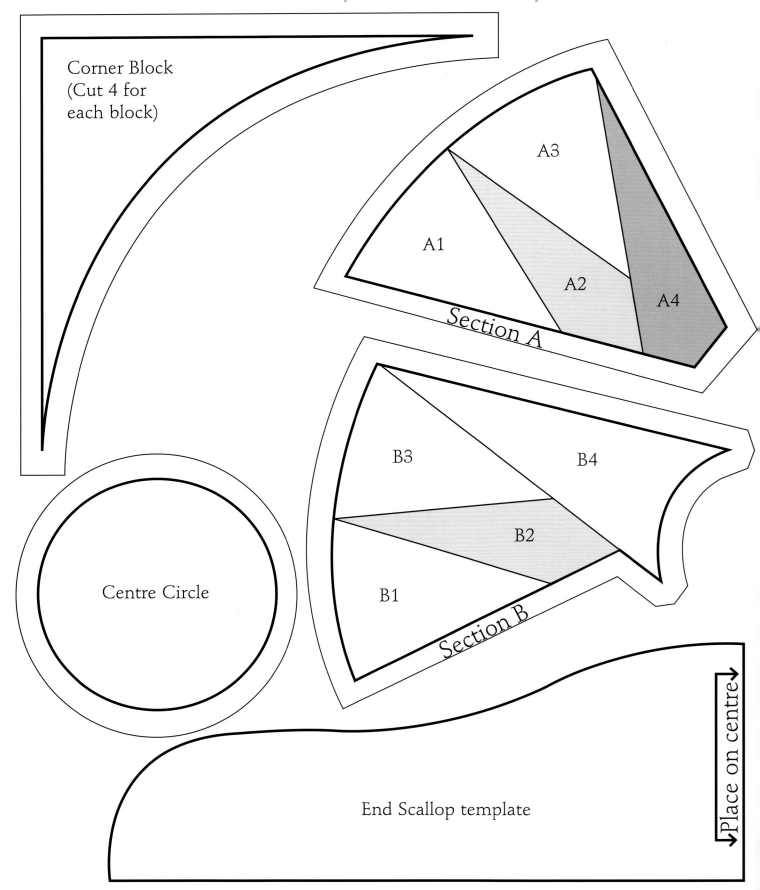

Sunflower Compass Placemat templates

Corner Block
(Cut 4 for
each block)

A3

A1

A2

A4

Section A

B3

B4

B1

B2

Section B

Centre Circle

Place on centre

End Scallop template

Mariner's Compass Tote Bag

Mariner's Compass designs can be round or square. This square compass block forms a star design in the centre. Even though it is a fairly small block, foundation piecing makes it easy to achieve perfect points. The bag is constructed in one piece with no inset sides or bottom gusset.

Cutting Instructions

From blue striped canvas, cut 1, 20-1/2" x 40-1/2" piece (for bag) on length of fabric.

From navy cotton, cut 2, 5" squares (compass block corners).

From cotton print, cut 1, 20-1/2" x 40-1/2" piece (bag lining).

Materials
60" (150 cm) wide cotton

Note: canvas used for this bag is sold in a wider width than regular quilting cotton. If using regular cotton you may wish to stabilize the fabric using an iron-on interfacing to give it extra body.

- 1.4 m (1-1/2 yards) of blue striped medium weight canvas (150 cm/60" wide)
- 0.6 m (5/8 yards) cotton print for lining (115" wide)
- 1.1 m (1-1/4 yards) fusible fleece batting
- 0.25 m (1/3 yard) each of 8 colours for the star: light yellow, medium yellow, light red, medium red, light gray, medium gray, light blue, medium blue
- 0.25 m (1/3 yard) navy cotton
- 3 m (3-1/4 yards) of 1" wide woven cotton straps (for bag handles)
- Sewing thread to match

Finished size: 16" x 18"
Block size: 8" square

From blue striped canvas, cut 1, 8-1/2" piece square (pocket lining).

To Make The Lining

Fold cotton print piece in half across the length, right sides together. The piece in front of you should now be roughly a square. Sew both side seams, leaving a 6" opening on one side seam for turning; do not turn right side out.

To make the flat bottom in the bag, measure 2" from side seam on bottom edge of bag and mark with a pin. Measure 2" up side seam from bottom of bag and mark with a pin. (figure 1)
Fold bag to match these pin marks, meeting the bottom of the bag to the side seam and pin in place forming a triangle. Measure up 2" from the bottom point of the triangle, pin,

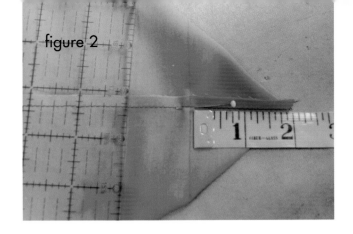

figure 2

and draw a straight line across. Stitch on this drawn line. (figure 2)
Repeat for other corner. Set lining aside.

Make 4 copies each of the supplied Mariner's Compass block foundation (page 105). Piece the block, referring to Foundation Piecing instructions in the General Directions. Place your colours as follows:

Section A:	Section B:
A1: light red	B1: Dark grey
A2 Dark Red	B2 Light Grey
A3: Navy	B3: Navy
A4: Light Blue	B4: Dark Blue
A5: Navy	B5: Navy
A6: Dark Yellow	B6: Yellow

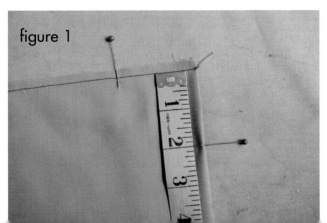

figure 1

When block is joined, carefully remove foundation paper.

Cut each of the 2, 5" navy squares in half diagonally. Sew one to each corner of the Mariner's Compass block. This block should measure 8-1/2". Square up as needed, and press. (figure 3)

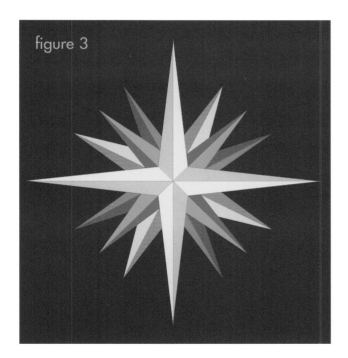

figure 3

Place 8-1/2" square canvas pocket lining on top of the Mariner's Compass block, right sides facing and sew to top and bottom edges, leaving sides open. Turn to right side and press. These raw side edges will be covered by bag straps.

Apply the fusible fleece to the back of the 20-1/2" x 40-1/2" striped canvas following manufacturer's instructions. Centre the pocket on the stripe print canvas 3-1/4" down from top edge and 6" in from each side. The finished edges of the pocket should be placed top and bottom with raw edges parallel to side of bag. Topstitch along raw side edges and across bottom of block through all layers to attach the pocket. (figure 4)

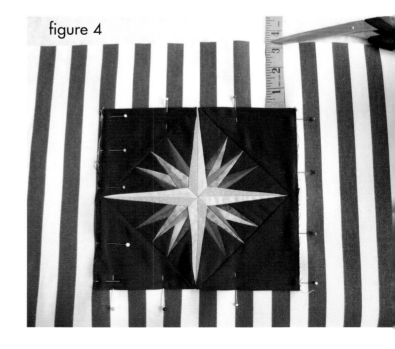

figure 4

Fold bag in half lengthwise to mark the bottom of the bag and press. Seam the red straps along short ends to form a loop and press seam open. Divide the strap in half from this seam and mark with pins; match these pins to the bottom of the bag. (This will place the joining seam on strap on the bottom of the bag.) Straps are placed 5" in from outside edge, which will just cover the raw edge on the Mariner's Compass pocket block. Be careful not to twist the straps. Straps will extend beyond the top and bottom of the bag forming a loop for the handle. Pin securely. (figure 5)

With matching thread, topstitch along the length of both sides of the straps through all layers to within 1" of both top edges of the bag. This leaves room to sew around top when attaching lining.

Fold bag in half, right sides together, and stitch both side seams. Make flat bottom as per the lining by measuring and marking 2" from side seam and on bottom edge of bag, matching pin marks as before. Measure up 2" from the bottom point of the triangle, pin, and draw a straight line across. Stitch on this drawn line. Repeat for other corner. Turn tote

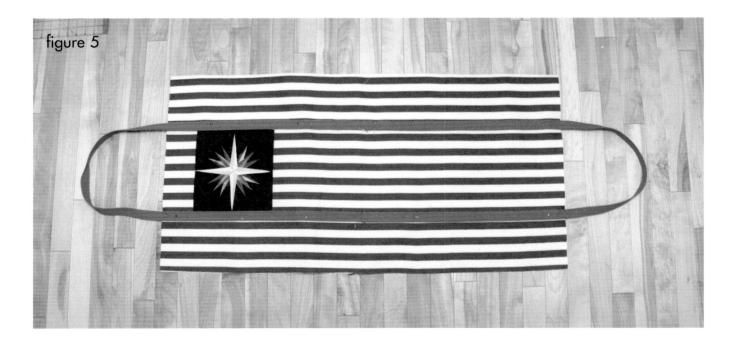

figure 5

104

bag right side out. Slip the tote bag inside the lining, right sides facing, making sure the straps are slipped between the lining and the tote. Stitch completely around top edge, being careful not to catch the straps in the stitching. Turn to right side through the opening in the lining. Slipstitch lining opening closed with a few hand stitches. Press seam at top of bag, ensuring lining is neatly inside, and finish topstitching the straps to the bag the final 1" from the top. Lay bag flat and press creases 2"

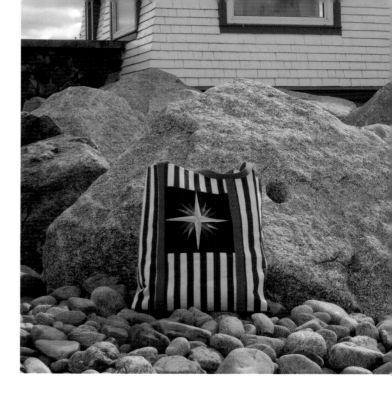

from each side seam and from bottom edge. This will help your bag stay flat.

Mariner's Compass Tote Bag Foundation

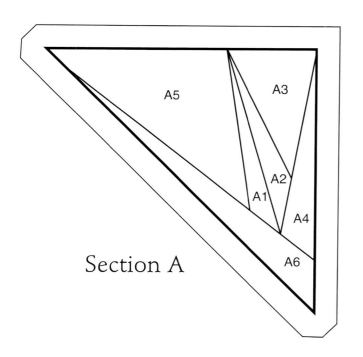

Section A

A5

A3

A2

A1

A4

A6

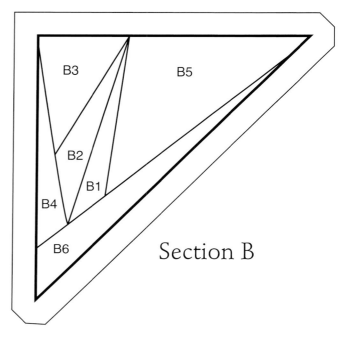

Section B

B3

B5

B2

B1

B4

B6

Redwork summer spread, c.1900, 63" x 68" (173 x 185 cm)

Redwork Quilts

Popular at the turn of the 20th century, embroidered scenes using floss and the stem stitch were known as redwork. In quilt blocks the typical subjects were botanicals, foods, animals (often owls) and other objects significant to the maker's life. The tufted summer spread shows the typical combination of flowers, animals, birds, and unusual designs. The design of a lady in winter was taken from an advertisement in the 1888 issue of Ladies Home Journal.

The embroidery was usually done in a true red colour called Turkey Red or oiled red. This red dye invented in Turkey did not run. Design patterns for pillow shams, tablecloths, towels and laundry bags could be purchased or traced from advertisement designs in newspapers and magazines. Pre-stamped fabric squares could be purchased for one cent, hence the name penny squares. Some of these embroidery pieces found their way into quilts. Pillow shams done with a variety of sayings such as "Good Night" were also very popular.

In past generations it was customary for girls to prepare for housekeeping by filling a hope chest, or "bottom drawer" with quilts and linens, which they had personalized with embroidery. The needle arts of crocheting, knitting, embroidery, and tatting, in addition to appliqué and patchwork, were developed and housekeeping items were gathered in preparation for marriage.

Redwork pillow sham, c.1900, 30" x 20" (76 x 51 cm)

Redwork Strippy Quilt

This frequently reversible design uses strips of fabric to construct a pieced quilt top and is believed to have originated in Northern England. Emigrants to Newfoundland and New Brunswick brought this piecing technique with them. In central New Brunswick the strippy design is called a ribbon quilt. It can be identified by wonderful quilting stitches executed in contrasting coloured thread on the uneven number of vertical fabric strips.

This looks deceptively like hand embroidery, but is done completely on a sewing machine. Freezer paper, available in grocery stores, has a waxy coating on one side which can be ironed to fabric and then peeled off. The white freezer paper is easier to see through than the brown when tracing, so check the colour of your paper when purchasing. Since the design is on the paper there are no marks to remove from the fabric afterwards. The heavyweight thread which is used to form the design is wound onto the bobbin.

Cutting Instructions

From white, cut 24, 6-1/2" x 12-1/2" blocks.

From red print, cut 5, 6-1/2" x 72-1/2" strips

From freezer paper, cut 24, 6-1/2" x 12-1/2" pieces.

Directions (figure 1)

Trace plume design (page 111) onto smooth side of freezer paper using permanent marker. Iron waxy side of the freezer paper to wrong

Materials
45" (115 cm) cottons

- 2 m (2-1/2 yards) white-on-white print
- 2.25 m (2-1/3 yards) red print
- 7.5 m (8-1/3 yards) binding
  (or 0.5 m [5/8 yards] of red print fabric
  to make binding)
- 4 m (4-1/2 yards) backing fabric
- 150 cm x 200 cm (60" x 80") batting
- 3 spools red silk thread, #30 weight
  (topstitching thread)
- Regular sewing thread
- White freezer paper
- Black sharpie marker, fine point

Finished size: 54" x 72"
Block size: 12" x 6"
Number of blocks: 24

figure 1

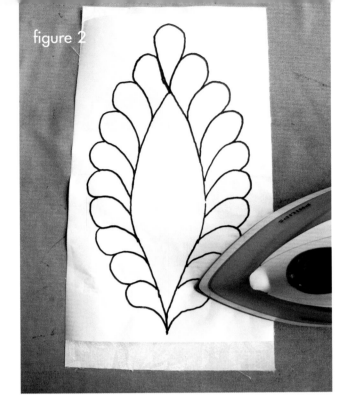

figure 2

side of fabric, centering the plume vertically and horizontally. (figure 2)

Turn fabric over and press right side of fabric smooth.

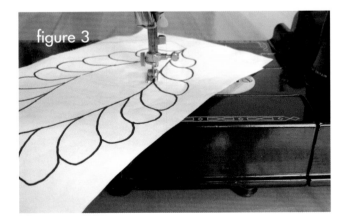

figure 3

Fill bobbin with red topstitching thread; use regular weight sewing thread in the top of the machine. Use a fairly long stitch length, around 10 stitches to the inch. Stitch along

drawn lines on paper with fabric side next to the machine and the paper on top. (figure 3) When stitching is complete, pull thread ends to wrong (paper) side; tie and clip. Carefully remove paper from around stitches. Repeat for remaining 23 blocks.

Sew 6 redwork blocks together on short ends to form 1 long strip measuring 6-1/2" x 72-1/2". (figure 4) Repeat to make 4 long strips.

figure 4

Sew patchwork and red print strips

figure 5

together in alternate rows, one row of plumes
heading up, the next row heading down.
(figure 5) Press seams toward the
red print.

Layer, baste, and quilt.
Trim edges even; bind.

Redwork
Strippy
Plume
design

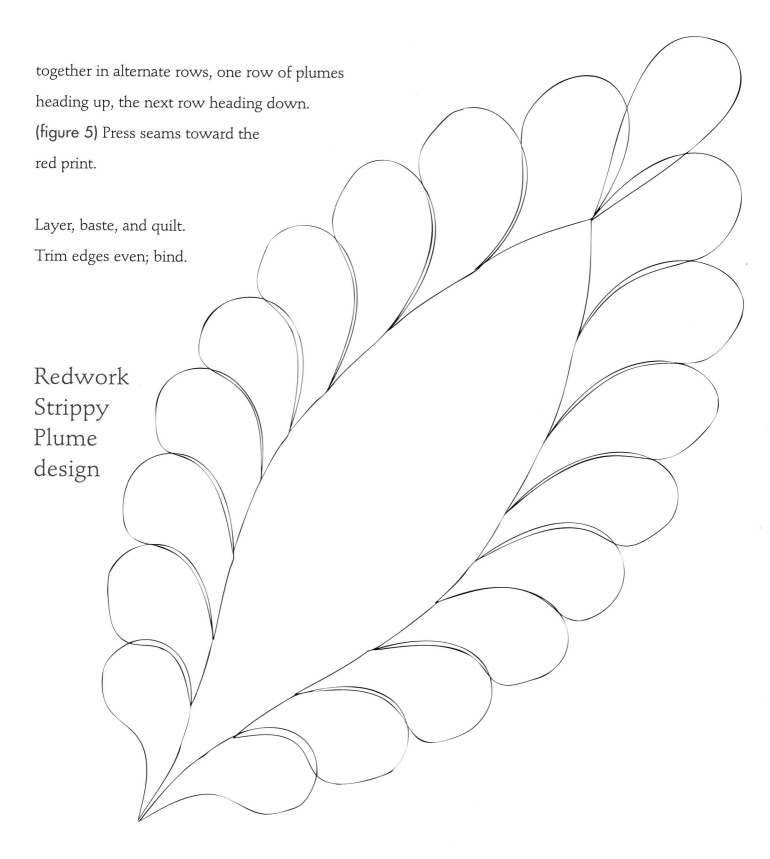

Appliqué Quilts

Appliqué or laid-on work involves decorative stitching, sometimes called fancy or needlework. The fabric designs with the raw edges folded in are laid on and stitched down to a background fabric. Quilt historians believe that generally more appliqué quilts have survived but records at provincial museums in Saint John, NB, and Halifax, NS, indicate that this is not the case for the Atlantic Provinces. Their collection records show ratios of appliqué to pieced quilts of 1:10. It is thought that women of Atlantic Canada were too busy and did not have the extra money for fabrics to do fine appliqué work.

The common type of appliqué done in the early 19th century uses a repeated design done in block format. The appliqué technique is the most realistic method to portray detailed designs. Appliqué patterns for designs, such as Sunbonnet Sue and the Butterfly, were available in Canada soon after they were created in the 1920s in the United States. These designs could be ordered by mail from most newspapers, but the clever quilter made her own patterns. In the 1930s the most popular method of attaching fabric to backing was to use a black blanket stitch. More elaborate appliqué, featuring invisible appliqué stitches in matching coloured thread, occurred in the mid-19th and returned in last part of the 20th-century. Today the technique is further simplified with the use of fusible web and state-of-the-art sewing machines that make fancy stitches.

Trapuntoed (stuffed) Appliqué, c.1885, 74" x 84" (188 x 213 cm)

WINS quilt, c.1940, 64" x 83" (162 x 211 cm)

Top: Tulip quilt, c.1962, 64" x 79" (162 x 200 cm)
Above: Lace postcard, WWI

This appliquéd tulip quilt, made in Nova Scotia, was received as a wedding gift in 1962. The group who did the hand stitching on the plain blocks chose to leave the appliquéd blocks unquilted which caused the cotton batting to clump together after washing. The edge finish cut on the bias was used because of the ease of attaching it to the curved edges.

Over a hundred years ago the Women's Institute was formed to educate rural women in all aspects of homemaking. They distributed patterns and designs, thus promoting the art of quilting. The logo of the Women's Institute of Nova Scotia (WINS) and motto "For Home and Country" was appliquéd using solid colours. Quilts made in Eastern Canada can often be identified by the use of a large amount of white and solid colours.

Postcards were one of the few ways to communicate during the early 20th century. The delicate lace postcard (above left) made its way from France during World War I to Five Islands, NS. It was sent by Austen Davis to his soon-to-be bride, Myrtle Patterson. As well as a record of a friend's activities and travel, the imagery is a study of designs of the time. Those more artistically inclined quilters who use fibre and thread to express their creativity have adopted mail art as a form of miniature appliqué. Postcard fibre art can go through the normal postal service.

Postcards from the Maritimes

Lighthouses from each of the three Maritime Provinces, in three distinctive styles, have been selected for these postcards. Each is trimmed in the corresponding provincial tartan. They can be mailed as is, just like a regular postcard using peel-and-stick stamps, or sent inside an envelope for extra protection. Check with your local post office to have them weighed and hand-cancelled.

L to R: Gannet Rock, NB; North Rustico, PEI; Five Islands, NS

Directions

Apply fusible web to back of background (sky print) and fuse to 4-1/2" x 6-1/2" stabilizer. Leave edges rough, they will be trimmed to size after the stitching is complete. Apply fusible web to back of appliqué fabrics and cut out pieces using patterns supplied (pages 116-117). Arrange the designs on the stabilized background print and fuse in place. Using matching thread and a narrow machine satin stitch (zigzag), stitch around each piece. Add stitching detail lines as indicated to form doorways, yellow beacons, windows, and gulls. When stitching is complete, pull thread ends to back. Tie and clip.

Apply fusible web to plain cotton fabric for backing. Remove paper from web, centre, and fuse to back of postcard. With rotary cutter, trim edges so postcards measure 4" x 6". Apply bias binding.

Materials
45" (115 cm) cottons
for one postcard (individual variations listed separately):

- 6-1/2" x 4-1/2" background (sky) print
- 6-1/2" x 4-1/2" plain white cotton or muslin for backing
- 6-1/2" x 4-1/2" firm stabilizer (such as Timtex®, or Stitch N Tear®)
- 0.25 m (1/3 yard) paper-backed fusible web
- 1.5 m (1-2/3 yards) tartan bias binding
- Thread to match fabrics
- Black permanent marker (such as a Sharpie)

For Five Islands, NS, Lighthouse:
- 6-1/2" scraps of white, red, green, grey, blue print fabrics

For North Rustico, PEI, Lighthouse:
- 6-1/2" scraps of white, red, green, stone print fabrics

For Gannet Rock, NB, Lighthouse:
- 6-1/2" scraps of white, blue, stone print fabrics

Finished size: 4" x 6"

Lighthouse Postcard templates 4" x 6" each

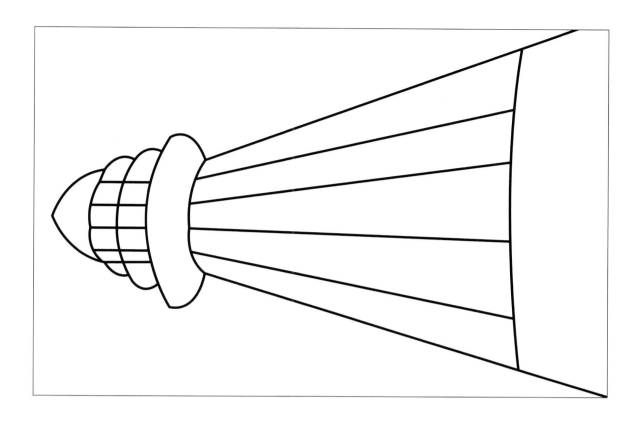

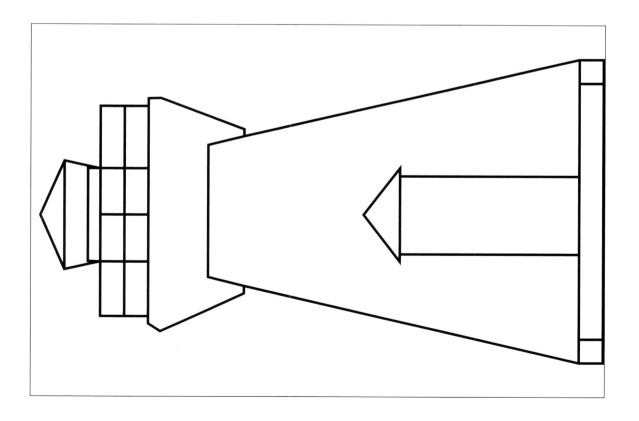

In Apple Blossom Time Quilt

Spring comes very late to the Atlantic Provinces. In the Annapolis Valley of Nova Scotia, the Apple Blossom Festival is held the first weekend in June when fruit trees are in full bloom. In Apple Blossom Time combines appliqué with patchwork. The appliqué pieces are made by the "faced" method: fabric pieces are sewn right sides together with a lining fabric and turned, before being stitched to the background. Using this technique, raw edges are dealt with before doing the hand stitching.

Cutting Instructions

From blue fat quarters, cut a total of 24 assorted rectangles each 8" x 10".

From sky blue, cut 78, 2-3/4" squares (plain border blocks).

From sky blue, cut 35, 3-1/2" squares (quarter-square triangle border blocks).

From sky blue, cut 4, 3-1/4" squares (corner triangles).

From dark blue, cut 35, 3-1/2" squares (quarter-square triangle border blocks).

From brown, cut 2 pieces, 41-1/2" x 1-3/4" along the length of the fabric (top/bottom inner borders).

From brown, cut 2, 45-1/2" x 1-3/4" pieces along the length of the fabric (side inner borders).

From remaining brown, mark diagonal lines 1" apart on the bias (a 45° angle) on a single layer of fabric. You will need a total of 125" of 1" strips.

Draw a second set of lines on the bias 1-1/2" wide for total of 80". Cut on the drawn lines.

From light pink, cut 9, 2-3/4" squares (border).

From dark pink, cut 3, 2-3/4" squares (border).

Working on the dull side of freezer paper trace designs with pencil, following instructions on the templates. Cut on solid lines of paper templates. Place each paper template, shiny side down, on wrong side of the appropriately coloured fabric. Iron in place with the shiny side of the freezer paper against the wrong side of the fabric.

Materials

If possible choose batiks, hand-dyes or marbleized fabrics with a variety of shades and gradations of the same colour.

- 1.5 m (1-2/3 yards) or 6 fat quarters various shades of blue
- 0.7 m (3/4 yard) sky blue
- 1.25 m (1-2/3 yards) brown for tree branches and inner border
- 0.5 m (5/8 yard) variegated greens for the leaves
- 0.25 m (1/3 yard) light pink
- 0.25 m (1/3 yard) dark pink
- 0.5 m (5/8 yard) solid green for lining leaves and bud stems
- 0.5 m (5/8 yard) solid pink for lining flowers
- 3 m (3-1/4 yards) quilt backing
- 3 m (3-1/4yards) batting
- 0.5 m (5/8 yard) fabric to make 4.5 m binding
- Freezer paper
- 1 package of pearlized stamens from craft supply outlet
- Pink, green and brown silk thread for appliqué
- Sewing and quilting thread to match

Materials for Appliqué

Glue stick, appliqué needles, silk pins, tweezers or medical clamps, iron and small scissors if desired.

- Finished size: 56-1/2" x 49-1/2"
- Number of blocks required: 16 centre blocks; 70 QST border blocks
- Finished size of blocks: centre blocks 7-1/2" x 9-1/2"

QST border Blocks: 2.25"

The following appliqué flowers and leaves are cut with a 1/4" seam allowance around each piece.

From brown, cut 6 B-1 sections and 10 B-2 sections.

From dark pink, cut 6 large flowers A-1, 6 buds A-3, 6 centres A-6.

From light pink, cut 3 flowers A-2, 10 buds A-4, and 6 centres A-5.

From green, cut 15 G-1 leaves, 10 G-2 leaves, 12 G-3 leaves, 5 G-4 leaves.

Sewing Directions

Centre rectangles for background are joined first and the appliqué is worked on this section. Once the appliqué is complete, the borders are added to the quilt.

Sort blue 8" x 10" rectangles into a pleasing arrangement and lay out in rows, 6 blocks across and 4 down. Sew blocks together in rows, then sew rows together. Press seams to one side. Patchwork measures 38-1/2" x 45-1/2".

Place right sides of backing (lining fabric) together with right sides of appliqué pieces. With matching thread, machine stitch all around paper template staying just outside the paper. Cut out leaving 1/4" around all shapes, clipping almost into stitching in curved areas. Press.

Remove freezer paper template and cut tiny slit in centre of lining material. Turn the appliqué piece inside out by pulling the right side to the outside through the slit. Tweezers are useful in this process.

Smooth out pieces and press so backing is not visible.

Make bias stems from brown bias-cut strips by folding strips into thirds with raw edges on inside. Press. Width of stems can vary from 1/2" to 3/4".

Place brown bias stems on a diagonal across the blue blocks in a pleasing arrangement.

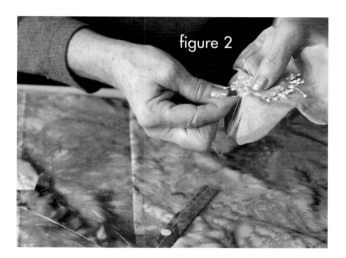

Refer to pictures for suggested placement of elements. (figure 1)

Sew pink buds to brown bud stems. Arrange 10 stamens in center of large blossoms, cover with one of the small circles and hand stitch to large flowers. (figure 2)

Green leaves with raw ends should fit under the stems. Use glue stick to hold pieces in place.

Using an invisible appliqué stitch and silk thread in a matching colour, sew stems to blue background. (figure 3) Sew leaves in place and stitch buds and flowers to ends of stems.

Sew 1-3/4" x 45-1/2" brown border to top and bottom of quilt. Sew 1-3/4" x 41-1/2" brown borders to sides. Press.

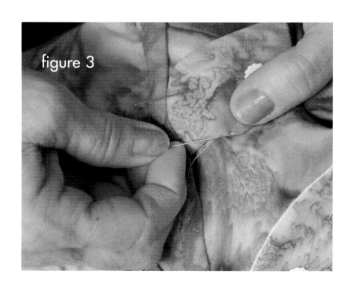

To make pieced border blocks: Place 35, 3-1/2" sky blue squares on top of 35, 3-1/2" dark blue squares; refer to General Directions to make 70, QST blocks. Trim the blocks to 2-3/4" square. Using diagram as a guide, sew QST blocks alternating with plain sky blue and pink 2-3/4" squares. If desired, pieced blocks may be randomly turned for interest. There are 21 blocks used in each row of the top and bottom borders. Sew rows together in pairs and add borders to top and bottom of quilt.

Cut the 4, 3-1/4" sky blue squares diagonally in half, corner to corner forming 8 triangles. Place these triangles at the ends of the side border strips to create an angled corner. The inner rows of the side border have 20 plain blue and QST blocks alternating, plus a triangle on each end. The outer rows of the side borders have 18 plain blue and QST blocks alternating, plus a triangle on each end. Press all borders away from quilt. Your pieced top measures 57" x 50" at this point. Layer top, batting and backing; baste and quilt as desired. Sample shown uses a one-inch grid in the background and outline

around designs. Veins were quilted in the leaves with green thread. Trim quilt edges even; bind. If desired, quilt may be embellished with purchased pins or buttons of bumblebees.

In Apple Blossom Time templates

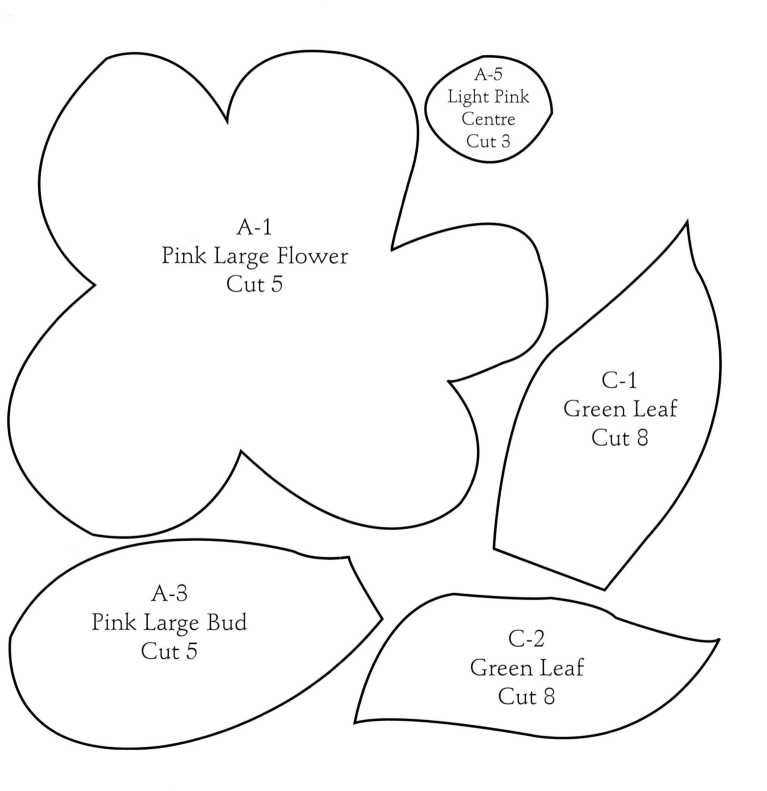

A-5
Light Pink
Centre
Cut 3

A-1
Pink Large Flower
Cut 5

C-1
Green Leaf
Cut 8

A-3
Pink Large Bud
Cut 5

C-2
Green Leaf
Cut 8

In Apple Blossom Time templates

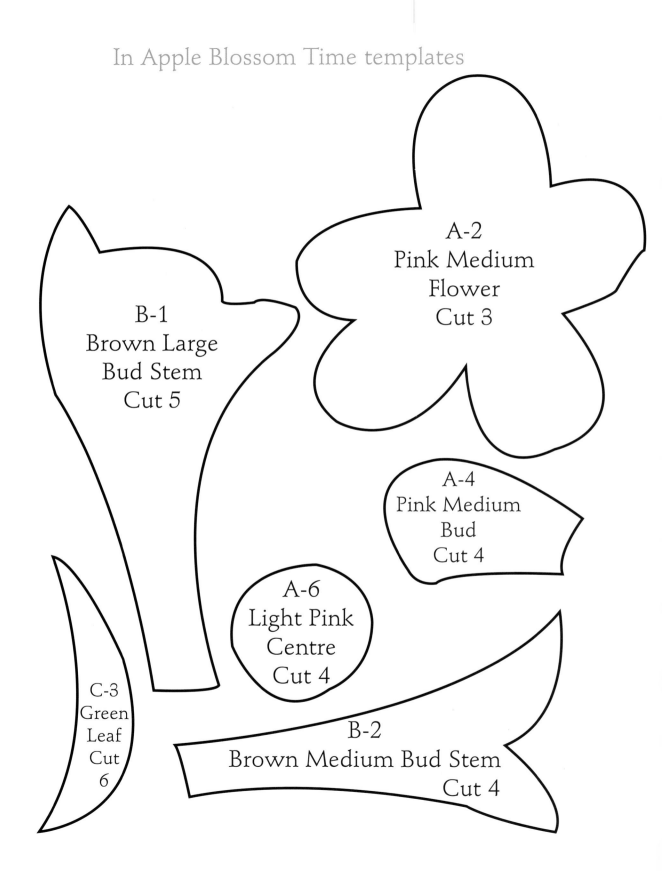

B-1
Brown Large
Bud Stem
Cut 5

A-2
Pink Medium
Flower
Cut 3

A-4
Pink Medium
Bud
Cut 4

A-6
Light Pink
Centre
Cut 4

C-3
Green
Leaf
Cut
6

B-2
Brown Medium Bud Stem
Cut 4

Epilogue

Many of the quilts shown in this book have survived because they have been stored properly and gently used, made before electric washing machines and hot water heaters were available. It has been said that the agitator in an electric washing machine combined with the extravagant use of chlorine bleach has caused the early demise of thousands of quilts. In the days of hand washing, dark wool quilts were washed at the end of the winter, if at all, and were put into the laundry tub at the end when the water was cool.

 ## Top ten things you should know about caring for your quilt

1. The ideal way to store quilts is flat on beds, a maximum of five per bed. Most museums use the rolled storage method. If you store them folded or fanned, air and re-fold at least twice a year. Old sheets or acid free paper can be used to pad the folds.

2. Quilts displayed on walls should be stored flat for as long as they hang, recommended six months vertical and six months horizontal.

3. Wooden rods or display racks should be sealed so wood does not put out gases which could cause colour change or deterioration. Use a double sleeve so the quilt will not come into direct contact with the hanging apparatus. The weight of the quilt should be evenly distributed across the quilt.

4. Light and dirt are quilts' biggest enemies. Protect them from direct sun or have UV protection installed on your windows.

5. Quilts should be clean before storage. All quilts will benefit by a light vacuuming, especially wool and silk, which should not be washed. Dry cleaning is not recommended.

6. Natural fibers need to breathe. Cotton sheets, pillowcases, and washed muslin are great for storing quilts and protecting them from edges of chests, trunks, etc. Plastic bags are a no-no.

7. Attics and basements are not good places to store quilts. 50% humidity and 10-15° C (50-60° F) temperature is recommended for ideal storage conditions. Dirt, high heat, moisture, and extreme cold cause fabric deterioration.

8. Stains should be treated and rips and tears repaired before cleaning. Sometimes spot cleaning will be enough, using enzyme-based stain removers and gentle soap. A double binding, cut on the bias, is recommended to extend the life of quilts made to be used as bedcovers.

9. Cotton quilts can usually be carefully wet cleaned (washed). The process should be done in a large space, use the tub of a washing machine as a vessel, fill with water, add cleaner and allow to soak, DO NOT AGITATE. Rinse on gentle cycle. When possible spread quilt flat to dry, out of direct sunlight.

10. If in doubt about cleaning methods consult an expert. Do not do anything that cannot be undone. Some antique quilts are best left untouched. You may reduce the value of the quilt by improper cleaning or restoration.

Bibliography

Citrigno, Jo-Ann and Lambert, Jennifer, *Needle Arts in Nova Scotian Women's Lives*, Nova Scotia Museums, Halifax, 1998.

Conroy, Mary, *300 Years of Canada's Quilts*, Griffin House, Toronto, 1976.

Duke, Dennis, and Harding Deborah, *America's Glorious Quilts* Park Lane, New York, 1989.

Eaton, Linda, *Quilts in a Material World*, Winterthur, Abrams, New York, 2007.

Eddy, Celia, *Quilted Planet*, Clarkson Potter, New York, 2005.

Harding, Deborah, *Red & White American Redwork Quilts*, Rizzoli, New York, 2000.

Horton Laurel, *Quilt Making in America, Beyond the Myths*, American Quilt Study Group, Rutledge Hill Press, Nashville, 1994.

Marler, Ruth, *The Art of the Quilt*, Courage Books, Philadelphia, 2001.

McCullough, A.B, *The Primary Textile Industry in Canada*, Parks Canada, Ottawa 1992.

McGinnis, Eddie, *Feed Sacks. Beautiful Quilts from Humble Beginnings*, Kansas City Star, Kansas City, 2006.

Mckendry, Ruth, *Quilts & Other Bed Coverings in the Canadian Tradition*, Van Nostrand Reinhold, Toronto, 1979.

Mountain Mist Blue Book of Quilts, Stearns Textile Co., Cincinnati, 1996.

Neering, Rosemary, *The Canadian Housewife*, Whitecap Books, Vancouver, 2005.

Nephew, Sara, *Quilt Designs from the Early Thirties*, Dover Publications, New York, 1988.

Orlofsky, Patsy and Myron, *Quilts in America*, Abbeville Press Inc., New York, 1992.

Oslerm, Dorothy, *North Country Quilts: Legend and Living Tradition*, Bowes Museum, Barnard Castle, England, 2000.

Rae, Janet, *The Quilts of the British Isles*, Constable, London, 1987.

Robson, Scott, and MacDonald, Sharon, *Old Nova Scotian Quilts*, Province of Nova Scotia, Halifax, 1995.

Rubio & Waterson eds., *The Selected Journals of L.M. Montgomery*, Volumes II & III, Oxford University Press, Toronto, 2000.

Shaw, Robert, *Quilts: A Living Tradition*, Hugh Lauter Assc., Westport, 1994.

Stark, Dee, *A Spiderweb for Luck*, self published, 2003.

Walker, Marilyn I., *Ontario's Heritage Quilts*, Boston Mills, Erin, 1992.

Wilson, Wood, *The Frenchy's Connection*, Pottersfield Press, Lawrencetown, 2001.

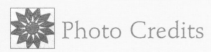 Photo Credits

l = left, r = right, t = top, c = centre, b = bottom
Photos were taken by Karen Neary, with the exception of the following: Alex Brzezinkski: 14t, 70, 73, 107, 121, 122; Morrow Scott Brown: 4, 22t, 62b, 86; John DeFusco: 63; Rob Johnstone: 1, 61t, 6b, 12, 13, 20, 21, 30, 31b, 47, 60, 61, 62t, 94, 95tr, 113; Marilyn Greshorne: 118; New Brunswick Museum: 5, 61, 95t, 112.
Quilt collections property of Diane Shink or Karen Neary, with the exception of the following: Emily Drysdale (70, 73); Fraser Cultural Centre (62r); Anne Kaufman (14); Barbara Ross Mackenzie (21); New Brunswick Museum (95b, 112); Chris Sontag (86); Mary Beth Sutherland (61, 62t); Sammy Treen (22tl); Ruth and Art Weatherby (1, 95r).

Index

(page numbers in italics refer to illustrations)